Ripley's
Believe It or Not!®
PRESENTS

SIDESHOW
— AND OTHER —
CARNIVAL CURIOSITIES

Ripley
PUBLISHING

Vice President, Licensing & Publishing Amanda Joiner

Editorial Manager Carrie Bolin

Editor Jessica Firpi

Designer Scott Swanson

Feature Contributors Engrid Barnett, Jessica Firpi, Jordie R. Orlando

Factchecker Katherine Bontrager Houlehan

Proofreader Rachel Paul

Reprographics Bob Prohaska

Cover Artwork Scott Swanson

Published by Ripley Publishing 2020

10 9 8 7 6 5 4 3 2 1

ISBN 978-1-60991-334-2

For more information regarding permission, contact:
VP Licensing & Publishing
Ripley Entertainment Inc.
7576 Kingspointe Parkway, Suite 188
Orlando, Florida 32819
publishing@ripleys.com
www.ripleys.com/books

Manufactured in China in November 2019 by Leo Paper

First Printing
Library of Congress Control Number: 2019951471

PUBLISHER'S NOTE
While every effort has been made to verify the accuracy of the entries in this book, the Publisher cannot be held responsible for any errors contained in the work. They would be glad to receive any information from readers.

WARNING
Some of the stunts and activities are undertaken by experts and should not be attempted by anyone without adequate training and supervision.

Ripley's
Believe It or Not!®
PRESENTS

SIDESHOW
AND OTHER
CARNIVAL CURIOSITIES

PUBLISHING

a Jim Pattison Company

CONTENTS

"THE WORLD IS ROUND,
BUT A LITTLE BUMPY."

— ROBERT RIPLEY

STEP RIGHT UP

Globally renowned as the authority on the weird, the eccentric, and the amazing, Ripley's Believe It or Not! is proud to present the true stories behind some of the most fascinating acts in historical and modern sideshow.

From displays of the human form—both beautiful and grotesque—to tricks of illusion and wonders from the far-off world, the sideshow has captivated audiences since its popularity arose in the Victorian era (1837–1901). The term "sideshow" entered the lexicon in the mid-1800s when P. T. Barnum popularized the word, which means a show featured on the side stages of circuses, fairground midways, and exhibition halls.

Sideshows and dime museums were a natural progression of the freak shows that captivated England in the 1750s. People considered "freaks of nature" (those with unusual physical characteristics, genetic anomalies, and attention-grabbing performers, like sword swallowers) fascinating and, unlike today, an acceptable form of entertainment.

But not everything was real. Circus impresario P. T. Barnum began his career in 1835 by exploiting an elderly slave named Joice Heth, branding her the "161-Year-Old Woman" and touting that she was George Washington's wet nurse. The lies made Barnum an estimated $1,500 a week.

Barnum ran his American Museum from 1841 to 1868, featuring other hoaxes like the Fiji mermaid, among other odd exhibits, and showcasing people like General Tom Thumb, who stood just 25 in (63.5 cm) tall when he first met Barnum. Many "freaks" and sideshow performers made a name for themselves with Barnum's help or as part of Barnum's menagerie. Thus, his stake in carnival curiosities can't be overstated. There can be no doubt that the "Prince of Humbugs" was a great showman—some would say the greatest.

From the 1880s through World War II, with easy access from New York City, Coney Island was a major vacation destination. In its heyday, nothing was too eccentric, too big, or too outlandish. Three major parks—Luna Park, Steeplechase Park, and Dreamland—all competed for visitors and the bigger the better, taking advantage of the public's captivation with the unknown. The famous venue has seen its fair share of performers grace its sideshow stages.

But freak-show and sideshow performers were ostracized in society, as evidenced by the public's reaction to director Tod Browning's 1932 film *Freaks*, which featured real performers of the era. The movie was a critical and commercial failure, effectively ending Browning's career and sending audiences screaming in terror. It was banned in various countries for decades before finding its audience in the 1960s, when it became hailed as a cult classic.

The very first Ripley's Believe It or Not! museum at the 1933 World's Fair in Chicago saw an astounding two million visitors. Inside the "Odditorium" were dozens of Ripley's famous cartoons, hundreds of strange and exotic artifacts Ripley acquired from his worldly travels, and of course, the strangest live performers ever gathered under one roof. The Odditorium sensation swept the nation, with popular appearances at world expositions across the country. Nevertheless, the company got out of the live performance business shortly after Robert Ripley's death in 1949.

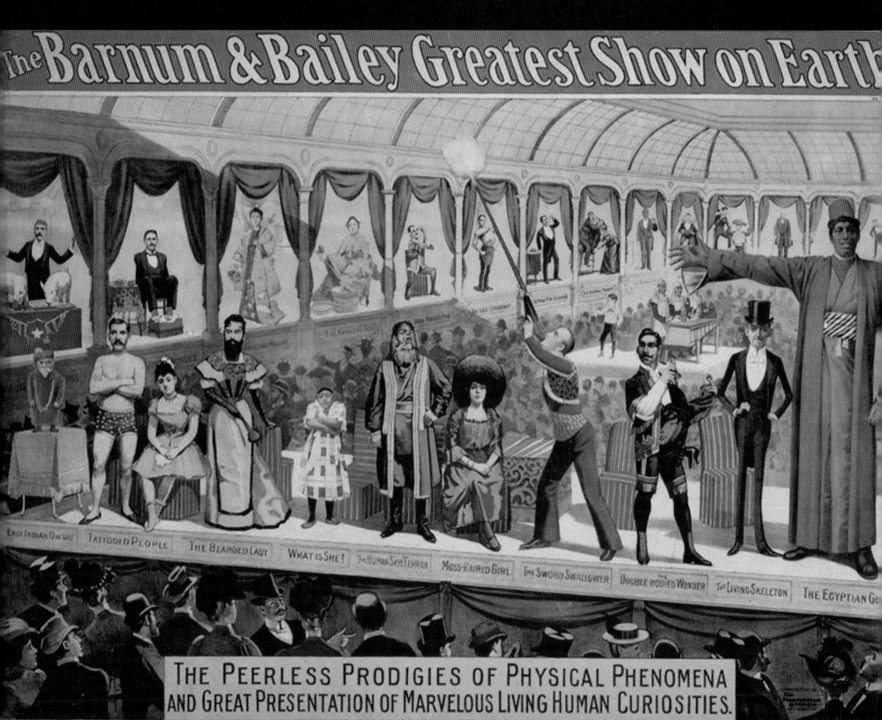

The ethics of sideshow have always been questionable. Over time, the public has had a change of heart regarding the exploitation of disabled performers for profit and fame—turning from indifference to outrage. Even the display of non-Western cultures and races, not to mention the blatant facsimiles that flooded the industry, has rightfully seen its end.

States began to outlaw the exhibition of people with disabilities, and by the end of the twentieth century, the "freak show" slowly died out. Shows like those at Ripley's Odditoriums in the 1930s and 1940s are a bygone phenomenon... or so one would think.

While many have enjoyed and decried the Coney Island freak show, it still exists today. Against all odds, Sideshows by the Seashore is the last permanently housed nonprofit venue in the United States where professional performers showcase traditional sideshow acts.

Although many historical performers were unable to make career decisions independently, whether due to developmental issues, difficult circumstances, or even abuse, a fair few chose the sideshow life, happy to travel and entertain the masses with their unique abilities. The traveling lifestyle was a chance for those born different to escape and live with and be accepted by others like them. And despite any negative experiences, many became extremely rich and famous.

Modern-day performers keep the proud tradition of those who came before them. No longer bound by inferior circumstances, performers today choose the sideshow life and, just like many of their predecessors, are delighted to shock and amaze audiences.

Now, Ripley's invites you to step right up and experience this compendium of curiosities.

WORLD'S
GREATEST
LIVING
CURIOSITY

JOHN ECKHARDT JR.

STAGE NAME: JOHNNY ECK

BILLED AS: THE MOST REMARKABLE MAN ALIVE; HALF BOY

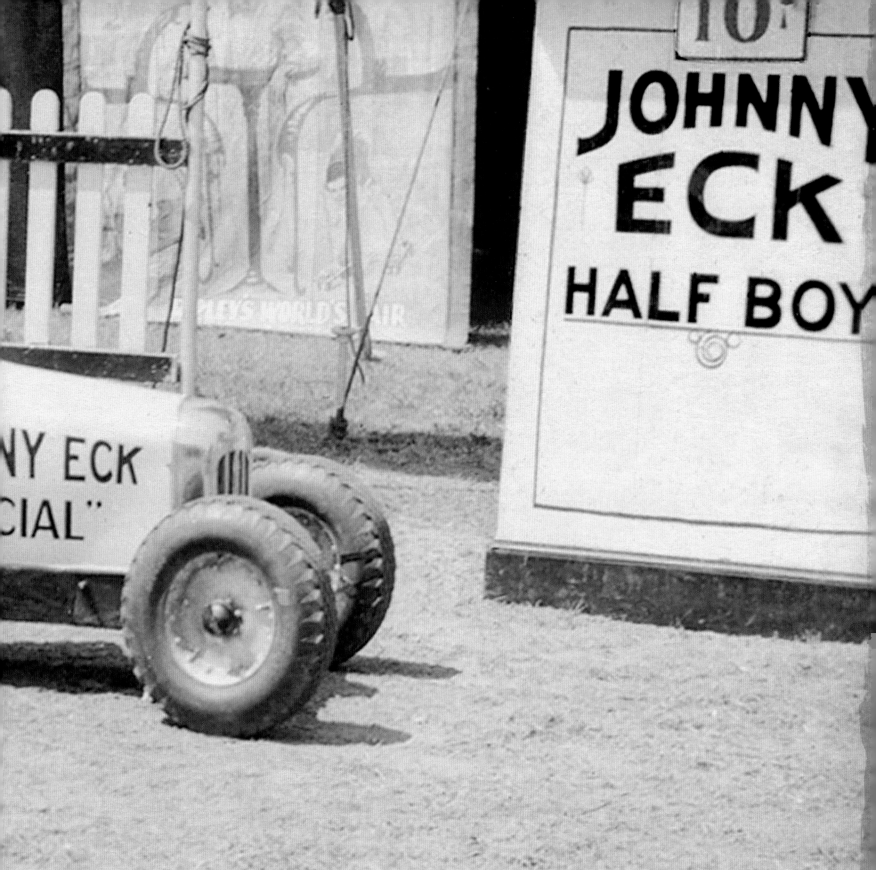

Born on August 27, 1911, John Eckhardt Jr.'s torso ended where his hips should have been, resulting in him being less than 8 in (20 cm) long and weighing 2 lb (0.9 kg) at birth. But that didn't slow him down—he began walking on his hands before his twin brother Robert was even standing.

JOHN ECKHARDT JR.

Johnny entered the sideshow world at age 12 along with Robert, his constant companion. Their most legendary act consisted of Johnny chasing a pair of legs (actually a dwarf hidden in a special pair of pants) around the stage after being "sawed in half" by a magician. They would run backstage, where they would be replaced by Robert, who would appear in front of the audience, seemingly whole again, and loudly threaten to sue the illusionist.

Here is Johnny during the "sawed in half" routine.

Johnny famously appeared in Tod Browning's 1932 film *Freaks* as Half Boy. Soon afterward he could be seen at Ripley's Believe It or Not! Odditoriums at the 1933 Chicago World's Fair, earning enough money to keep from losing his childhood home during the Great Depression.

Johnny and Robert eventually retired and moved back to their hometown. The brothers built and operated a miniature train for the neighborhood children, and Johnny became a screen painter. He passed away at the age of 79 on January 5, 1991, in the same house where he was born.

GREATER TEXAS AND PAN AMERIC

Acct. No. 601   Pass N

Employee of Oddities, Inc

Name   John Eck

Signature   *John Eck*

1937   IDENTIFICATION

VALIDATE FOR   *H. S. Karr*

JULY
                AUTHORIZED SIGNATURE
AUG.
                AUTHORIZED SIGNATURE
SEPT.
                AUTHORIZED SIGNATURE
OCT.

JULY   AUGUST

When asked if he wished he had legs, Johnny Eck reportedly quipped, "Why would I want those? Then I'd have pants to press."

AARON WOLLIN

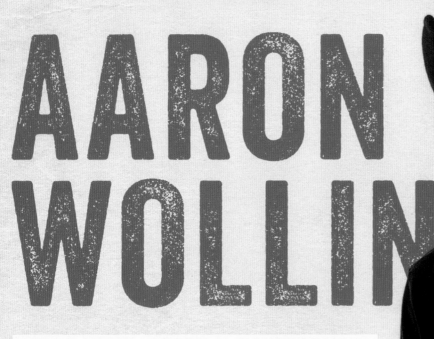

STAGE NAME: SHORT E. DANGEROUSLY
BILLED AS: "HALF-MAN"

Aaron Wollin (aka Short E. Dangerously) is a 21st-century half-man, wowing audiences with acrobatic feats, fire-breathing, and glass-walking— all on his hands.

Unlike Eck, one of his personal heroes, Short E. was born with legs, but a condition forced a double amputation when he was two years old. Before becoming a performer, Short E. was a nightclub DJ.

Now Short E. travels extensively with a sideshow troupe, performing not only acts similar to what Johnny did in the 1930s but also his own extreme stunts, like performing handstands on bowling balls and jumping from a chair onto a pile of flaming glass without being harmed. He says, "Johnny is a personal hero of mine. He paved the way for guys like me. I hope to live up to his legacy and surpass it at the same time."

"SIDESHOW IS MORE OF A LIFESTYLE AND WHEN I'M OUT ON TOUR IT CONSUMES EVERYTHING I DO."

Here Short E. is recreating Eck's famous one-arm balance.

ARNOLD GERRIT HENSKES

STAGE NAME: MIRIN DAJO
BILLED AS: THE HUMAN PINCUSHION

Mirin Dajo was born Arnold Gerrit Henskes on August 6, 1912, in Rotterdam, a city in the Netherlands. He became famous for his human pincushion routine, which consisted of him piercing his body with different objects, with no apparent ill effects.

Henskes was highly religious and meditated before an assistant named Johann de Groot shoved a fencing sword through his abdomen and then removed it, unbelievably drawing no blood. He adopted the stage name Mirin Dajo, which means "wonder" in the Esperanto language.

In the late 1940s, Henskes did shows where shocked audience members would pass out as Henskes walked around impaled by a sword. His pincushion routine did not go unnoticed, and various hospitals and doctors studied and witnessed his act. At one point, Henskes even jogged around with the 28-in (71.1-cm) blade still in his body. The medical community was only left with more questions than answers, as X-rays revealed that the sword did run right through his body, piercing several internal organs, and caused no internal bleeding when removed. This was no magician's trick.

Today, it's likely that Henskes was not necessarily invulnerable. His Swiss performance troupe included a hypnotist, so it's possible that hypnotism or his meditation helped block the pain, not that he was immune to it. And if Henskes's assistant consistently and carefully inserted the blade along a line of scar tissue and his organs were pierced with a clean cut using a clean metal blade, then the risk of infection would be minimized and the wound nonlethal.

On May 11, 1948, Henskes ate a steel needle—which he allegedly claimed his guardian angel told him to eat—and a doctor surgically removed the needle a day or so later. More than a week after the surgery, Henskes laid down in his assistant de Groot's apartment, never to awaken. De Groot had assumed he was meditating, but after three days, he had no pulse. On May 26, 1948, he was pronounced dead, at the age of 35. The autopsy revealed the cause of death was a ruptured aorta.

MIRIN DAJO A DUTCHMAN

WHOSE NAME MEANS "SOMETHING WONDERFUL" PASSES A RAPIER THRU HIS BODY WITH **NO** ILL EFFECTS! HE CLAIMS TO HAVE STABBED HIMSELF THRU THE HEART WITHOUT HARM

"SOMETHING WONDERFUL"

Ripley's Believe It or Not! cartoon from May 4, 1948— just 22 days before Henskes passed away.

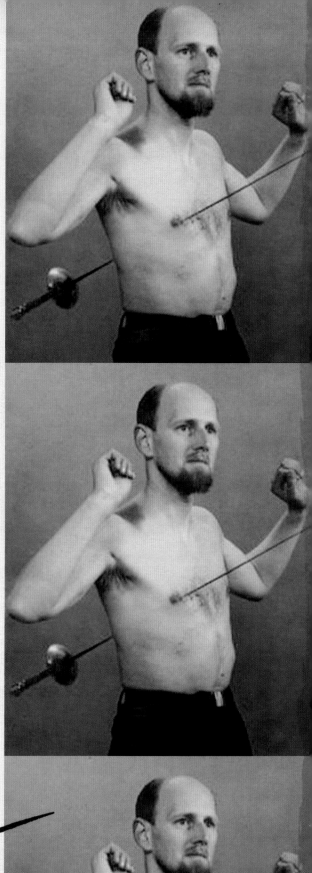

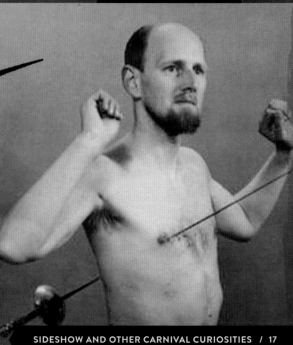

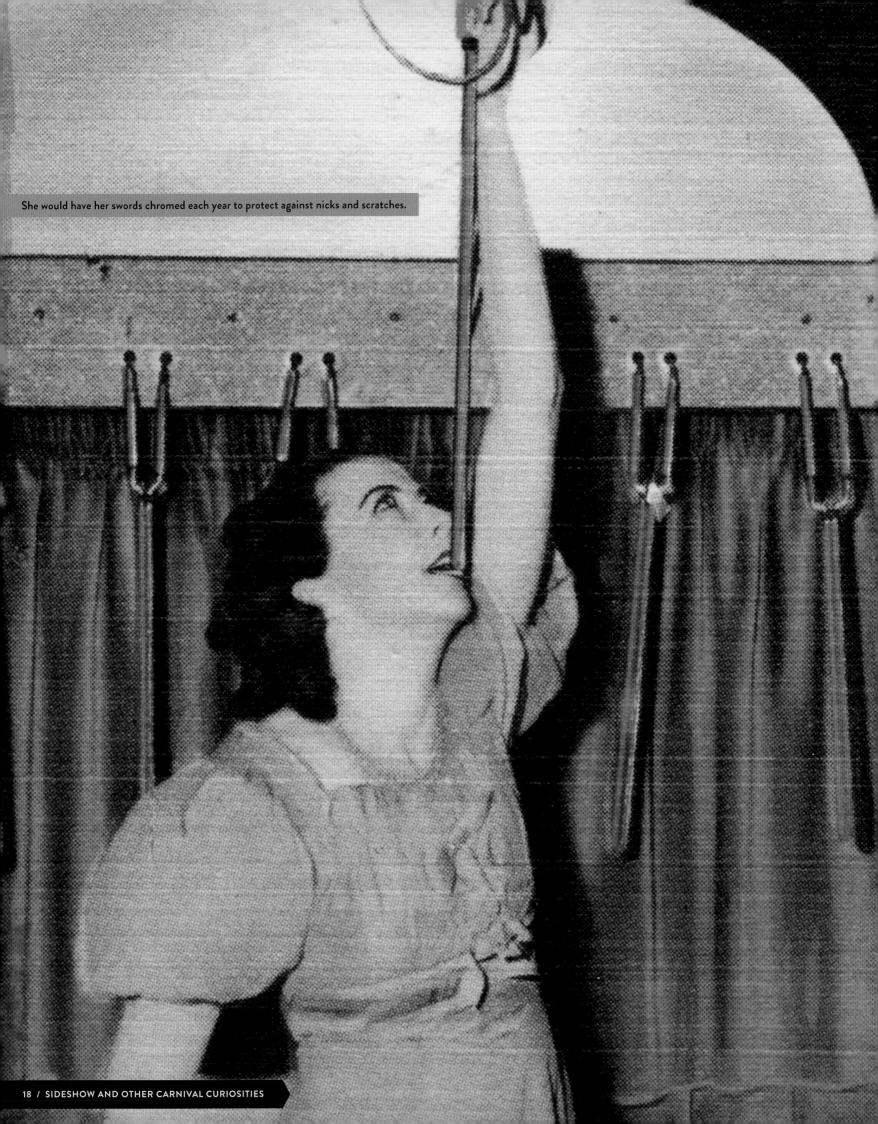

She would have her swords chromed each year to protect against nicks and scratches.

EDNA PRICE

BILLED AS: QUEEN OF SWORD SWALLOWERS

Hailing from a family of sword swallowers—her Aunt Maude had died after swallowing a sword for King George V of England in 1920—Edna Price was born for the circus, getting her start in the sideshow business at just 16. Her veteran sword swallower uncle, Delno Fritz, quickly trained her into a star. He taught her to sword swallow at age 20, and she soon joined up with the Ringling Bros. and Barnum & Bailey Circus alongside her uncle.

While they traveled around, Edna became a true daredevil and darling sideshow performer. It's even been noted that when she wanted to go out with a boy her uncle didn't approve of, that she would hide his wooden leg so he couldn't stop her. Though her uncle passed in 1925, Edna stuck with the circus and eventually became close friends with Major Mite and Harry Houdini.

In May 1933 at the Chicago World's Fair, Edna Price was one of the remarkable "human rarities and oddities" enlisted by Robert Ripley's talent spotters to appear at his show, where she would swallow 2-foot-long (0.6 m) neon tubes that glowed through her throat. Edna was also able to swallow 12 swords at a time, removing the blades one at a time. Robert Ripley proclaimed her the "Queen of Sword Swallowers."

She went on to perform at Ripley's New York Odditorium for the 1939–40 World's Fair and at Coney Island before retiring from sword swallowing to work at Ripley's Believe It or Not! in Atlantic City as a hostess.

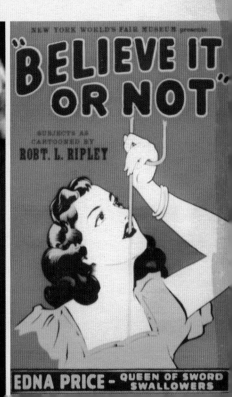

Stills from archival footage of Edna Price, "Queen of Sword Swallowers," swallowing a glowing neon tube.

CHARLES SHERWOOD STRATTON

STAGE NAME: GENERAL TOM THUMB

Performer and international celebrity, General Tom Thumb (named after the English folklore character) was born Charles Sherwood Stratton on January 4, 1838, in Bridgeport, Connecticut. By the time he was six months old, he had stopped growing, standing 25 in (63.5 cm) tall and weighing just 15 lb (6.8 kg)—although he later grew to 3 ft 4 in (1 m) and 70 lb (31.8 kg).

KENNINGTON, S.E.
TWO NIGHTS ONLY.
Wednesday & Thursday Evenings,
April 28 & 29.
GRAND FASHIONABLE MORNING PERFORMANCE
ON THURSDAY at 3.
Tickets to be had of Mr. J. Wilson, Stationer & Newsagent,
194, Kennington Park Road, and at the Horns Tavern,
where Specimens of the Presents may be seen.
Admission: Reserved Seats, **2s.** Unreserved Seats **1s.** Back Seats, **6d.**
Children under 12 Half-price to First and Second Seats only. Carriages ordered for 10 o'clock.

Recently patronised by the Crown Prince and Princess of Prussia and Family. Lady Gordon Lennox, and Lady Bryan.

UNEQUALLED COMBINATION

PROFESSOR MILLAR AND HIS LITTLE MEN.

KING OF LILLIPUTIANS

THE ORIGINAL AND ONLY AUSTRALIAN

GENERAL TOM
THUMB

THE SMALLEST WELL-FORMED MAN IN THE WORLD.

Handsome, perfect in form, well educated, has a voice as strong as any full-grown man; in appearance a mere speck of humanity, but in intellect a giant, and, altogether, the most remarkable person in existence.

The General was born in Melbourne, Australia, of European parents, both of whom were tall and large in bulk. Tom's brothers and sisters are rather above the average size of humanity, while our hero is not larger than a child four years of age, and in possession of all possible dignity. His intellect is astonishing, his powers of analysis keen and subtle, his perception acute and infallible, and his digestion marvellous. He sings, dances, acts, gesticulates, and vociferates, in a style for which the only expressive term is a pocket edition of the cleverest comedian. His impersonations of character are refined and cannot fail to please the most fastidious taste. He will appear in elegant and appropriate costumes as

Paddy Murphy, with Song and dance; Grandfather Whitehead, with Song of "Come along de;" Jack Brace, the Son of the Ocean, with the Sailor's Hornpipe; Captain Jenks, the Swell of the Period, with Comic Song; The Gay Scotch Highlander, with National Dance; Ben Battle, the Bold Soldier Boy, with Song.

THE WORLD-FAMED COURT DWARF AND JESTER,

COMMODORE
KNOTT

Recently of the Crystal Palace London. The most remarkable FUNNY LITTLE MAN ever known, 34 years old and only 23 inches high. He has a noble, fine, handsome, expressive face, and is the SMALLEST, as well as one of the best COMIC VOCALISTS in the World, and stands alone without a rival.

£2000 PREMIUM

TO ANY ONE WHO WILL PRODUCE THEIR EQUALS.

PROFESSOR

MILLAR

The great Original and World-renowned Illusionist, Prestidigitateur, Lecturer, and Traveller.
Forming the most Novel, Truthful, Effective, Funny, Startling, Humorous, Instructive, Amusing, and Liberal Entertainment ever presented.

PROFESSOR MILLAR'S DAUGHTER,

MISS NELLIE MILLAR

SOLO PIANISTE AND MUSICAL CONDUCTRESS.

The Grand Oblique Cottage Pianoforte used at these Entertainments is manufactured by the celebrated maker, M. Feruck, of Leipsic, and may be had from William Lea, Church Street, Liverpool, Sole Agent for Great Britain.

Every detail will be found complete, every accessory to give effect will be applied, and the comfort of the Audience will be the earnest consideration of the Manager.

COSTLY PRESENTS GIVEN AWAY

The Manager begs to state that nearly all other Entertainments that distribute Presents are worthless, depending solely on the paltry trash they give away to attract and deceive. We wish it to be distinctly understood that our Seance is of superior excellence, and that we introduce the GREATEST NOVELTY IN THE WORLD.

At the Entertainment there will be GIVEN AWAY to the Audience a LARGE NUMBER OF COSTLY PRESENTS, exceeding anything ever attempted here, and will include Silver Watches, Silver plated Spoons, Breakfast and Dinner Casters, Tea Sets, Furniture, Gold Lockets, Silver-plated Goblets, beautiful Cameo Pins, Vest Chains, beautiful Silver-plated Tea and Coffee Service, Timepieces, Gold Rings, Silver Drinking Cups, Electro-plated Butter Coolers, Silver Cake Baskets, and many other rich, rare, and valuable articles too numerous to mention, forming the most costly number of gifts ever presented. The Manager having made arrangements with manufacturers, making very extensive purchases, is enabled to give elegant articles. Remember our presents are first-class, and not of a paltry kind. It will truly astonish all to see our splendid Presents; every one says, "How can they afford to give them?" We pledge ourselves to what we advertise, and guarantee the utmost satisfaction. PRESENTS GIVEN AWAY in that strictly honourable manner which has given universal satisfaction. Bear in mind NO EXTRA CHARGE FOR THE PRESENTS! The only charge is the price of admission to the Entertainment.

The Presents are Free.

TOM THUMB and COMMODORE KNOTT will make a Grand Parade in their beautiful miniature Brougham (manufactured expressly for them by Messrs. Wycherly & Son, Cheltenham), drawn by four splendid Goats.

To Persons going to America the Manager would recommend the GUION LINE U.S. MAIL STEAMSHIPS, sailing between Liverpool and New York, as the cheapest and best afloat. The Steamers of this Line have always called the safest route to New York. As a proof of this they have not lost one single Passenger by accident for over Twenty-five years. Tom Thumb, Commodore Knott, and Professor Millar have crossed by it several times.

AT EIGHT.

Agent in Advance, Mr. HARRY WILLIAMS.

Stratton with Barnum.

CHARLES SHERWOOD STRATTON

P. T. Barnum discovered Stratton when he was just four years old and quickly transformed him into a superstar, teaching him how to sing, dance, and do impersonations. He became a fixture in Barnum's American Museum in New York and then toured Europe in 1844, which is when Stratton first met Queen Victoria. He would eventually meet the queen three times, along with other European royalty.

In 1863, at the height of the Civil War, Stratton married the equally small Lavinia Warren. Another one of Barnum's performers, Lavinia was heralded as a miniature of perfect proportions, and the marriage was a major event in New York society. The happy couple stood on top of a grand piano in New York's Metropolitan Hotel to greet 2,000 guests at the reception. The best man at the wedding was "Commodore Nutt," yet another little person performing under Barnum's banner. President Lincoln even hosted the couple on their honeymoon.

Stratton's business partnership with Barnum flourished, and he amassed an immense fortune, including a stable of racehorses, a yacht, and a mansion decorated with miniature antique furniture. At one point, Stratton even bailed out Barnum's circus from financial ruin.

In 1883, six months after he survived a disastrous hotel fire that killed at least 70 people in Milwaukee, Charles Stratton suddenly died of a stroke. He was 45 years old. Thousands of people attended the funeral. Dying in 1919 at the age of 78, his wife Lavinia is buried beside him with a gravestone that simply says, "His Wife."

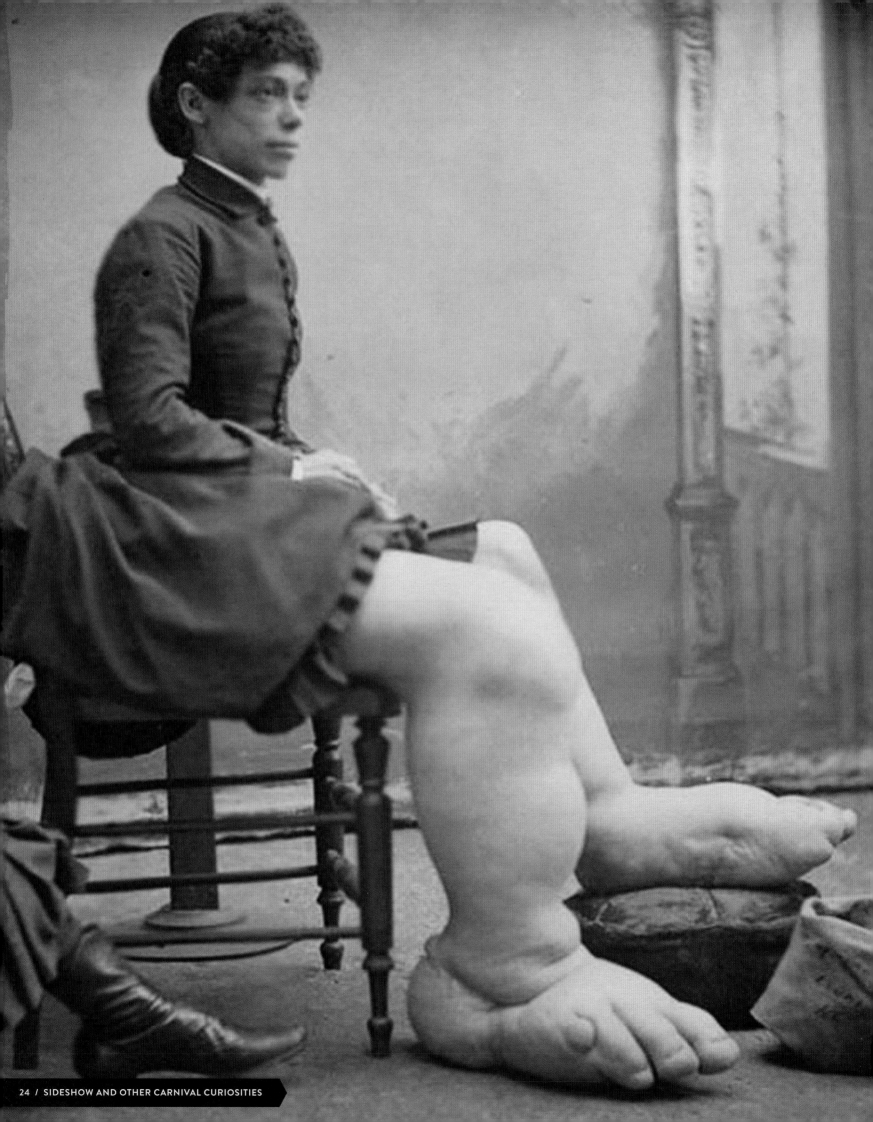

FANNIE MILLS

BILLED AS: THE OHIO BIG FOOT GIRL

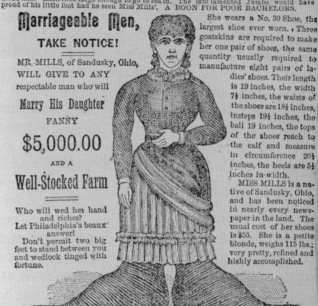

Born in Sussex County, England, in 1860, Fannie Mills had feet so large that she wore pillowcases for socks and her custom-made shoes were the equivalent of a size 30.

After immigrating to Sandusky, Ohio, with her parents, Mills joined the freak-show circuit in 1885, billing herself as "The Ohio Big Foot Girl." She weighed no more than 115 lb (52.1 kg) and sported a petite build, yet her feet proved enormous. They measured about 19 in (48.3 cm) and 7 in (17.8 cm) wide.

Why were her feet so large? Mills suffered from a rare condition known as Milroy's disease, caused by congenital abnormalities in the lymphatic system. Thus, she suffered from chronic lymphedema, a painful fluid buildup in her legs.

As a result of her condition, Mills found walking and standing to be excruciating, and she had difficulties completing daily tasks alone. She hired a nurse named Mary Brown to accompany and assist her.

To help Mills attract more viewers, her promoters devised a bizarre promotional ploy. They advertised that Mr. Mills, Fannie's father, was looking for a suitor for his daughter, and he was willing to pay a $5,000 dowry and provide a farm to anyone willing to claim her hand in marriage.

Although Mr. Mills never owned a farm and was deceased, the advertisement brought flocks of eligible bachelors to the sideshow. Soon, she pulled in $150 per week, making a fortune off the bachelors who meant to scam her. In 1886, she married William Brown, her faithful nurse's brother and a man who didn't require any financial incentives.

"MIDGET CITY"

Opened in 1904, Midget City, also known as the Lilliputian Village, was Coney Island's miniature town populated by more than 300 little people.

Villagers actually lived onsite and functioned like a community in their built-to-scale world. Even world-famous General Tom Thumb lived in Midget City with his wife. The residents had their own police and fire departments, a tavern, restaurant, theater, beach, and even performed their own acts, like the Tom Thumb Circus. For effect, the village would sometimes have "giants" walking around among them.

Showman Samuel Gumpertz, who helped build Coney Island's Dreamland, traveled the country looking for small people to live in Midget City. Many residents came from various World's Fairs, circuses, and freak shows.

About 60 little people were on display at a "midget exhibit" at the Chicago World's Fair in 1933–34. It was later expanded and officially called Midget City.

PASQUAL PIÑÓN

BILLED AS: THE TWO-HEADED MEXICAN

Born in 1889, Pasqual Piñón worked on the Texas railroad before a sideshow tour promoter helped him turn the benign tumor on his forehead into a revenue-generating second face.

Discovered in 1917, Piñón toured with the Sells-Floto Circus for several years gaining popularity as the "Two-Headed Mexican." But he lacked crucial characteristics associated with craniopagus parasiticus. This rare condition occurs when a parasitic twin's head and undeveloped body are attached to a developed twin.

In true cases of craniopagus parasiticus, like the two-headed boy of Bengal (1783–1787), the second head rests upside-down atop the main head. It often gesticulates or moves. But such was not the case with the immobile, gaping face on Piñón's forehead.

It turns out, the promoter fitted Piñón's benign tumor with a fake face. While some have claimed the head was made from silver and surgically implanted just beneath the surface of the growth, it's far more likely that it was a clever wax prosthetic.

Following a brief stint touring the country with the circus, Piñón's promoter paid for him to have the tumor removed. No one knows what became of Piñón following the surgery.

ELLA HARPER

BILLED AS: THE CAMEL GIRL

Ella Harper was born in Sumner County, Tennessee, in 1870 with congenital genu recurvatum—a condition that caused her knees to bend backward.

Walking on all fours was more comfortable for Harper, and she earned her "Camel Girl" moniker simply because she resembled a camel with her bent legs. By 1886, she was a prominent attraction with W. H. Harris's Nickel Plate Circus, often appearing alongside a real camel for emphasis and comparison. Her pitch card read as follows: "I have traveled considerably in the show business for the past four years and now, this is 1886 and I intend to quit the show business and go to school and fit myself for another occupation."

Indeed, her $200 a week salary helped her quit the sideshow business early, although not much else is known about Harper after her early retirement. She did marry in 1905 and in 1921, at the age of 51, died in Nashville, Tennessee.

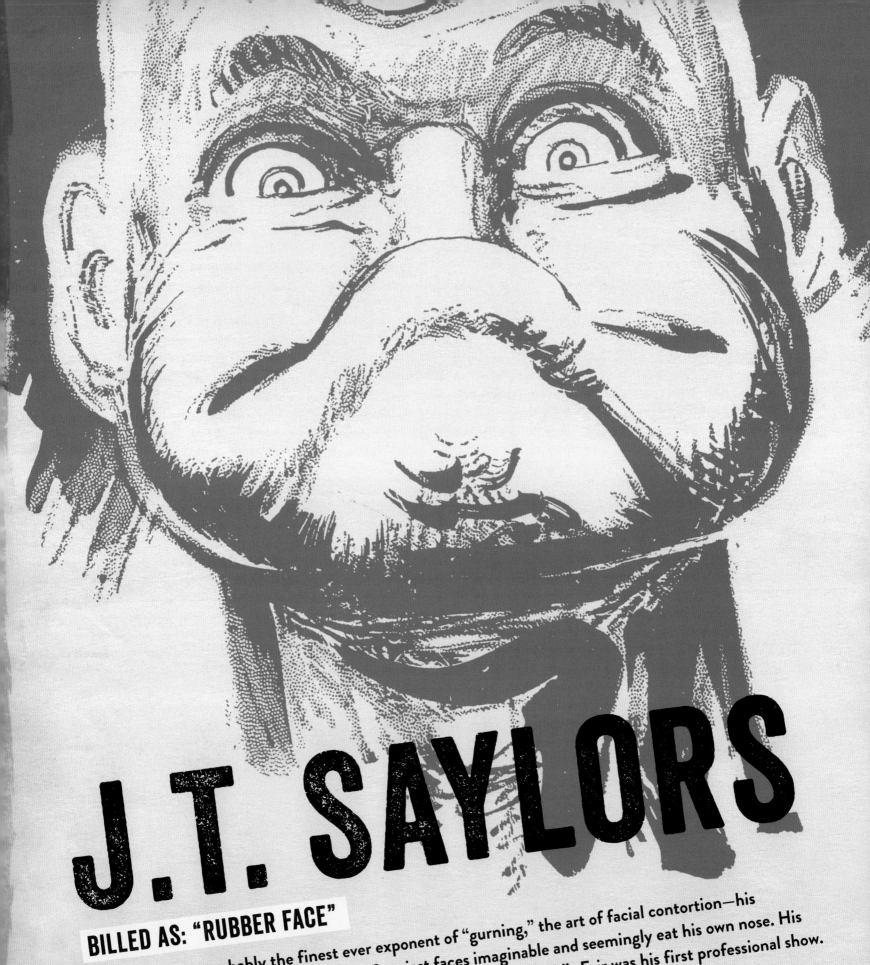

J.T. SAYLORS

BILLED AS: "RUBBER FACE"

J. T. Saylors was probably the finest ever exponent of "gurning," the art of facial contortion—his flexible jaws enabled him to pull off the funniest faces imaginable and seemingly eat his own nose. His performance at the Ripley's Odditorium at the 1933 Chicago World's Fair was his first professional show.

Robert Ripley featured Saylors in the famous Believe It or Not! cartoon.

OLD
FUNNY
FACE!

J.T. SAVLORS – of Villa Rica, Ga.
CAN DISLOCATE HIS JAWS
AND SWALLOW HIS NOSE

Gurning competitions are still taking place to this day, with the most famous being the World Gurning Championships held annually at Egremont, Cumbria, in England.

OR NOT
HE SWALLOWS HIS NOSE
HOMELIE MAN ON EAR
BOB WALLACE AS "OLD FUNNY FACE"

"BELIEVE IT OR NOT
HE SWALLOWS HIS NOSE
HOMELIE MAN ON EAR
BOB WALLACE AS "OLD FUNNY FACE"

"BELIEVE IT OR NOT
HE SWALLOWS HIS NOSE
HOMELIE MAN ON EAR
BOB WALLACE AS "OLD FUNNY FACE"

"BELIEVE IT OR NOT
HE SWALLOWS
HOMELIE MAN

BOB WALLACE

GRADY STILES JR.

BILLED AS: THE LOBSTER BOY

Grady Stiles Jr. came from a family afflicted for generations with ectrodactyly, where the digits on the hands and feet are spread apart and fused together, making them look like lobster claws. At a young age, his father added him to their circus act and so he began performing as "The Lobster Boy." But Stiles quickly earned a bad reputation on the sideshow circuit and later became infamous for murder.

Born in Pittsburgh, Pennsylvania, on July 18, 1937, Stiles's condition was so severe that he had to learn to use his hands and arms to get around. Although Stiles was unable to walk, he grew to be an abusive alcoholic, often beating his wife and his children. By 1978, Stiles and his first wife Mary Teresa had divorced, and he married a woman named Barbara.

His oldest daughter, Donna, who did not exhibit ectrodactyly, fell in love at a young age, and despite Stiles disliking her boyfriend, the two wanted to get married. The night before the wedding, Stiles shot and killed Donna's fiancé while she and her stepmom Barbara were outside looking for Stiles's wheelchair, which was somehow, for some reason, not inside the house. The boy died in Donna's arms.

Stiles confessed to third-degree murder, showing little remorse, and while the trial only lasted a few days, a reporter called it "one of the weirdest trials I ever covered." Character witnesses included a bearded woman and a circus "fat lady" who got stuck in the witness chair. Mary Teresa even attended the proceedings alongside her new husband, a little person who performed in sideshow as well. Believe it or not, Stiles did not serve any prison time for the murder, as the prison system could not accommodate a person with his special needs, not to mention his emphysema and cirrhosis of the liver.

Instead he received 15 years' probation, and moved to Gibsonton, Florida, where his ex-wife Mary Teresa was living; the two of them eventually divorced their spouses and actually remarried. Stiles resumed his abusive behavior, and in November 1992, he was shot three times in the back of the head while he was watching TV in his trailer.

It was determined that his wife and stepson had taken out a hit on him, paying another sideshow performer $1,500 to kill him. The hitman was sentenced to 27 years in prison, while Mary Teresa was sentenced to 12 years for conspiracy to commit murder. Mary's son Harry Glenn Newman III, from a previous marriage, was considered the mastermind, so he was convicted of first-degree murder and sentenced to life in prison.

Grady is buried with his father in the Showmen's section of Sunset Memory Gardens cemetery in Thonotosassa, just outside Tampa, Florida. The remaining members of the family still perform every so often.

CHANG WOO GOW

STAGE NAME: CHANG YU SING

BILLED AS: THE CHINESE GIANT

Born in the early 1840s in Fuzhou, China, Chang Woo Gow grew to nearly 8 ft (2.4 m) tall and entertained at both the royal court of the emperor of China and P. T. Barnum's "Greatest Show on Earth."

In 1864, the Prince and Princess of Wales requested that Chang (now Chang Yu Sing) leave the Chinese royal court for a visit to the United Kingdom. Chang proved pleasantly surprised by the fame and wealth awaiting him there.

Thousands of curious patrons flocked to see him, paying as much as three shillings each. What started as a brief visit to the United Kingdom expanded into a two-year tour of the country. During his act, Chang demonstrated proper Chinese etiquette and garb. Although he exhibited alone on many occasions, his act was sometimes combined with that of a dwarf to further enhance his incredible height.

Apart from his towering stature, Chang had an expansive intellect, quickly learning how to speak several languages, including French, German, and English. With his linguistic pursuits came an adoration of literature. He was known for always having a book on hand.

By 1881, he earned up to $600 per week working with Barnum, who billed him as "beautiful as Apollo" and "strong as Heracles." Although Barnum hired a Chinese woman named King-Foo to play Chang's wife on stage, this did not dampen the ardent devotion of his many female fans. During nearly every interview with the press, the number-one topic was his marital status.

Everything changed on a visit to Australia, where Chang met Catherine Santley of Liverpool. The two fell in love, got married, and had two sons together. After a brief stint in China, they settled in Bournemouth, England, where Chang retired from the sideshow world.

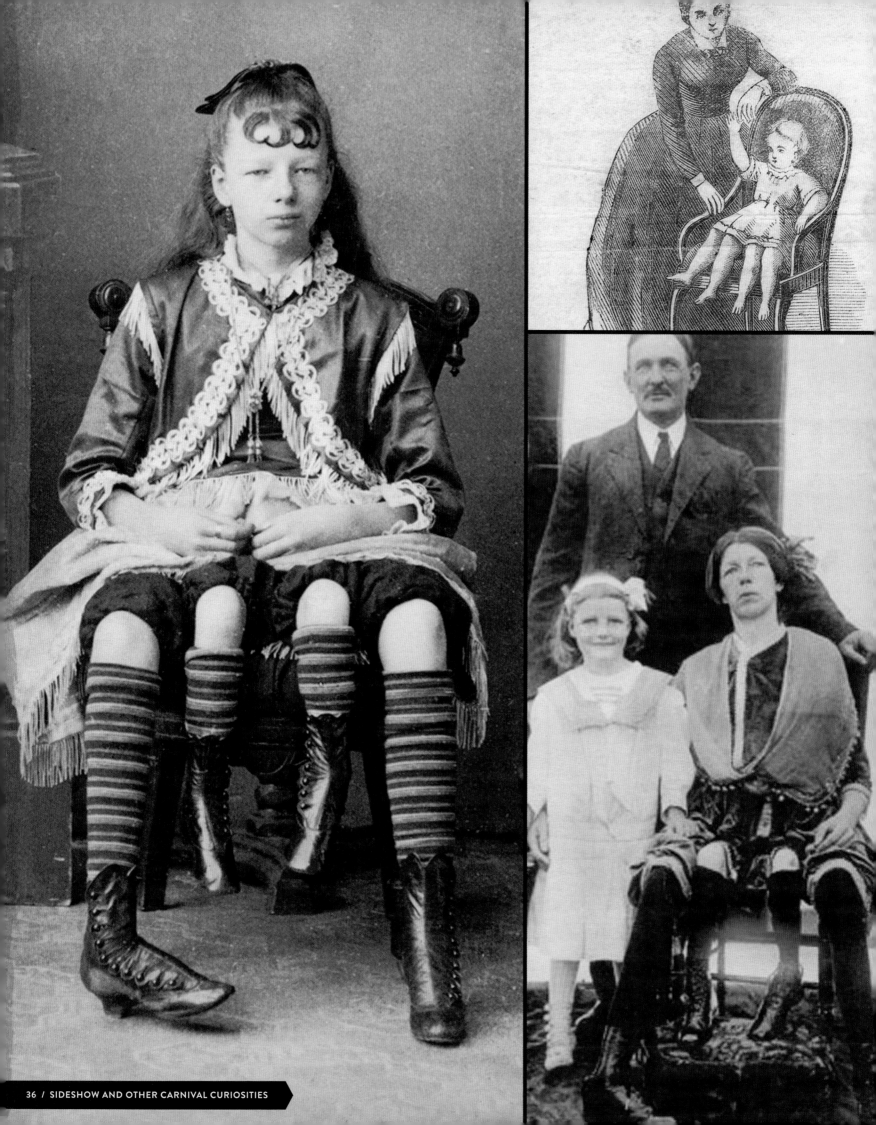

JOSEPHINE MYRTLE CORBIN

STAGE NAME: MYRTLE CORBIN

BILLED AS: THE FOUR-LEGGED GIRL

Josephine Myrtle Corbin was born in Lincoln County, Tennessee, in 1868, to normal, healthy parents who were not blood relatives, despite how closely they resembled each other with their red hair, fair complexion, and blue eyes.

Corbin exhibited a severe congenital deformity known as dipygus, where the body is duplicated from the waist down—so in essence, she had two separate pelvises side by side, each with their own two legs and sexual organ. Each outer leg was stronger and paired with a much-weaker inner leg. Although she could move all her limbs, she had a difficult time getting around, as she did have one clubbed foot and the inner legs were too frail to walk on.

It's said that her father began showing her to paying customers for a dime when she was just one month old. She eventually caught P. T. Barnum's attention, and thus, her sideshow career began. She started officially performing when she was 13, later with Ringling Bros. and at Coney Island.

Around this time, teratology—the scientific study of congenital abnormalities and abnormal formations—was at its peak, and there seemed to now exist a connection between the human exhibits of sideshows and medical science.

Doctor Brooks H. Wells wrote about Corbin in the *American Journal of Obstetrics*, describing her as a "female, belonging to the monocephalic, ileadelphic class of monsters by fusion." Of course, Corbin was no monster.

Her act, which consisted of her dressing the extra limbs with matching socks and shoes, was wildly popular. (In fact, she was so popular that many fake four-legged women were also exhibited during and after Corbin's career.) She was earning as much as $450 a week, and by the time she was 18, she'd made enough money to retire. At 19, she married a man named Clinton Bicknell, and just one year afterward became pregnant with her first child.

Although her first pregnancy made her ill enough to induce an abortion, Corbin did eventually have four children. Medical journals and doctors reveled in Corbin's pregnancies and unique anatomy, and today she's known in medical communities as "Mrs. B."

On May 6, 1928, Corbin died, surrounded by family and friends. Although doctors and collectors offered the family money in exchange for her corpse, she was buried and her casket was covered in concrete. Her family kept watch over the grave until the concrete was fully cured and grave robbers could never disturb her corpse.

FIJI
MERMAID

The Fiji mermaid is one of the most famous sideshow artifacts of all time—an ingenious hoax made from several apes (including possibly an orangutan and a baboon) and a fish, cleverly sewn together.

Its curious history dates back to the early 19th century, in the Dutch East Indies (modern-day Indonesia) where the mysterious beast was said to have been bought by a ship captain. The sailor believed that it was a genuine mermaid obtained in Japan and was so struck by the discovery, he paid an enormous sum of money to have it. On his return to London in 1822, he put the creature on public display as "A Mermaid, the wonder of the world!"

P. T. Barnum

On July 13, 1865, Barnum's American Museum on the corner of Broadway and Ann Street in New York City burned down. Although no one was killed, many animals perished, including two whales, which were boiled alive in their tanks.

FIJI MERMAID

With the field of marine biology somewhat limited, many people believed the mermaid was a genuine mummified mythical creature. But not everybody was convinced. *The Times* of London called for the animal to be dissected to authenticate it, noting that the upper torso and head of the creature looked exactly like a baboon's, and the tail, the skin, and the fins resembled that of a regular salmon. The skeptics were, of course, correct. Nevertheless, there was enough uncertainty about the real nature of the mermaid that it continued to attract visitors.

After the captain's death, the mermaid was sold to another showman who brought it in 1842 to the United States, where he persuaded the famous P. T. Barnum to put it on display at his American Museum in New York. His advertising material claimed that the mermaid belonged to a respected British doctor who had discovered it in the Fiji islands in the South Pacific. The "doctor" gave serious scientific lectures in which he claimed the mermaid to be a missing link between humans and fish. In fact, the doctor was also a fake—he didn't exist; he was actually a character played by one of Barnum's associates to make the mermaid seem more authentic. Any doubts raised over the mermaid's biology decades earlier in Britain had been forgotten, however, and the creature caused a sensation.

Barnum was still exhibiting the mermaid in the 1850s, but from that point on its history remains something of a mystery, and it was thought to have been lost in one of several fires that ravaged P. T. Barnum's collection. It lives on today in many Ripley's Believe It or Not! Odditoriums, presented as a crafty counterfeit.

Many years later, Robert Ripley unearthed a similar mermaid in a shop in Macau, Asia, and exhibited it at his New York Odditorium in 1939, although he always maintained that it was a clever fake.

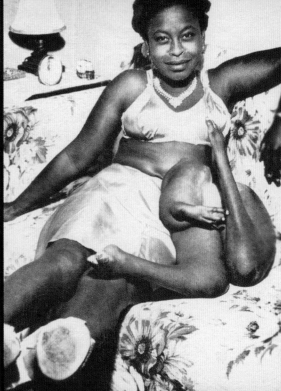

LILLIE B. WILLIAMS

STAGE NAME: BETTY LOU WILLIAMS

BILLED AS: THE GIRL WITH FOUR LEGS AND THREE ARMS

Born on January 10, 1932, to a large family of sharecroppers in Albany, Georgia, Betty Lou Williams became the highest-paid human oddity in history, due to an extra set of arms and legs protruding from the left side of her abdomen.

Christened Lillie B. Williams, she was the youngest of a dozen siblings. After hearing rumors of a four-legged girl in Georgia, Dick Best tracked her down for one of his exhibits. A professional showman, Best changed her name to Betty Lou and first displayed the one-year-old at his museum in New York.

People marveled at the miniature parasitic twin emerging from Williams's body. The attached sibling could be seen from the waist down and included an arm with three fingers, another tiny arm-like appendage, and two legs.

By the age of two, Robert Ripley negotiated with Best to show Williams for $250 per week. She debuted

Chicago World's Fair in 1934. According to Ripley, X-rays showed a perfectly formed head embedded deep within her abdomen. He billed her as the "Girl with Four Legs and Three Arms."

As Williams grew, so did her earnings. She sometimes dressed the twin in custom-made clothing and shoes. Soon, she brought in as much as $1,000 per week. With her earnings, she purchased a 260-acre ranch for her parents. She also helped each of her siblings go to college.

A kind and generous beauty, she had several ardent suitors. Yet, at the age of 23, she was jilted by her fiancé, who absconded with a large sum of her earnings. Despite the reassurances of doctors that Williams would lead a long and healthy life, she died unexpectedly in 1955 at her home in Trenton, New Jersey. Although her cause of death was listed as complications from an asthma attack, her friends maintained that she died of a broken heart.

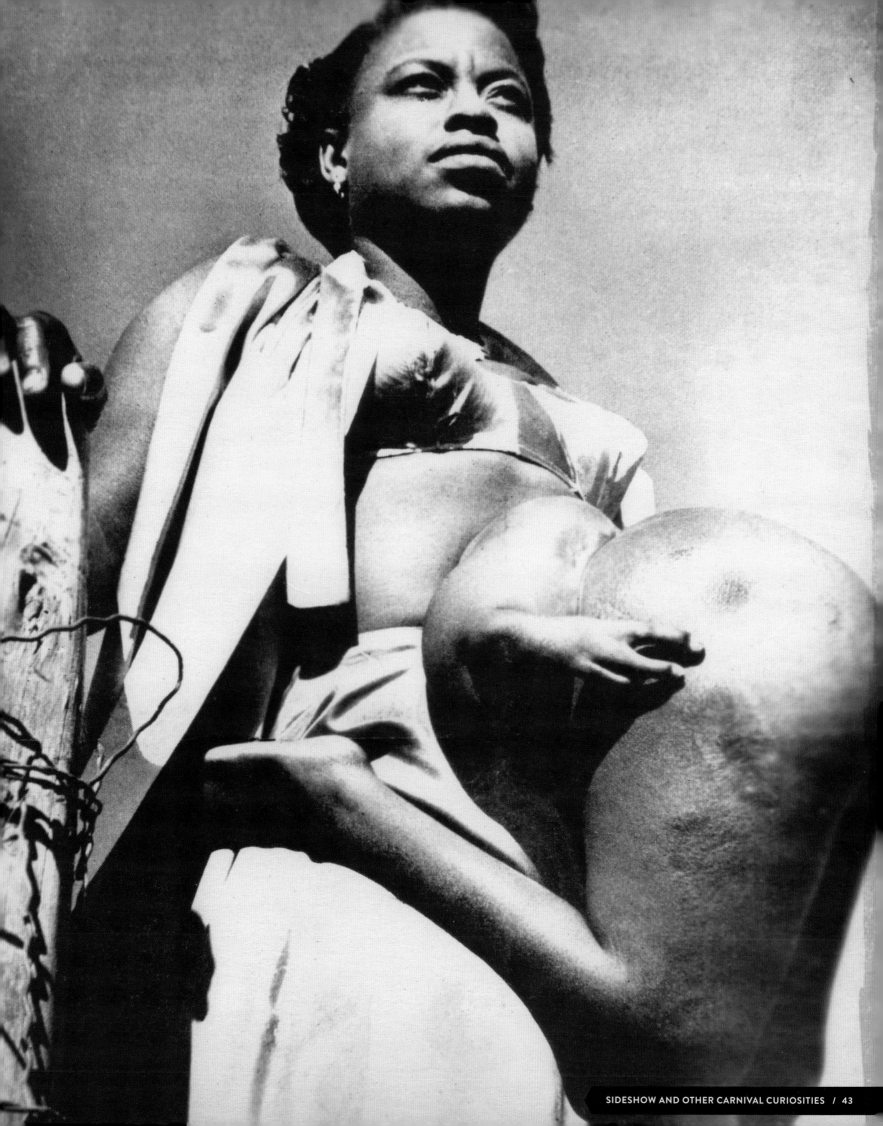

ELVIRA AND JENNY LEE SNOW

STAGE NAME: PIP AND FLIP

BILLED AS: PINHEADS; THE SNOW SISTERS

Famed for their heartwarming roles in the movie *Freaks* (1932), Pip and Flip, as they were known, were biological sisters who suffered from microcephaly.

Although billed as the sisters from the Yucatan, the Snow siblings hailed from Hartwell, Georgia. The older of the two, Elvira, was born on March 2, 1901, and Jenny Lee followed 12 years later.

Born with microcephaly, a neurodevelopmental disorder, each girl exhibited the same characteristics—abnormally small brains and craniums. Because their faces grew faster than their heads, they also had receding foreheads and small or "pin-like" heads. Besides these physiological impacts on their craniums, microcephaly also stunted their growth.

Elvira and Jenny Lee also experienced developmental delays. As a result, they had the mentality of toddlers. Their childlike innocence won them many fans. In *Freaks*, they starred alongside Schlitzie, another famous pinhead. From frolicking in the woods to dancing and being adorably bashful, Schlitzie, Elvira, and Jenny Lee endeared themselves to moviegoers.

At the height of their careers, the Snow sisters brought in about $75 per week, a significant sum during the Great Depression. Sadly, Jenny Lee died in her early twenties on August 27, 1934. But Elvira went on to live a long life, passing away on November 1, 1976, in a senior care facility.

ALFRED
LANGEVIN
THE MAN WHO SMOKES THRU HIS EYE

PLAYING
A FLUTE WITH
HIS EYE

NOW APPEARING IN THE ODDITORIUM

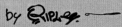

Believe It or Not!
by Ripley

ALFRED
LANGEVIN
THE MAN WHO SMOKES THRU HIS EYE

PLAYING
A FLUTE WITH
HIS EYE

NOW APPEARING IN THE ODDITORIUM

Believe It or Not!
by Ripley

ALFRED
LANGEVIN
THE MAN WHO SMOKES THRU HIS EYE

ALFRED LANGEVIN

Born around 1885, Alfred Langevin of Detroit, Michigan, could blow up balloons, smoke a cigarette, and play a recorder by forcing air out of his eyes.

He appeared at Ripley's Odditoriums from 1933 to 1940 and was featured in a cartoon as well as in a souvenir postcard for the 1940 New York City World's Fair Odditorium. Unfortunately, not much is else known about this performer.

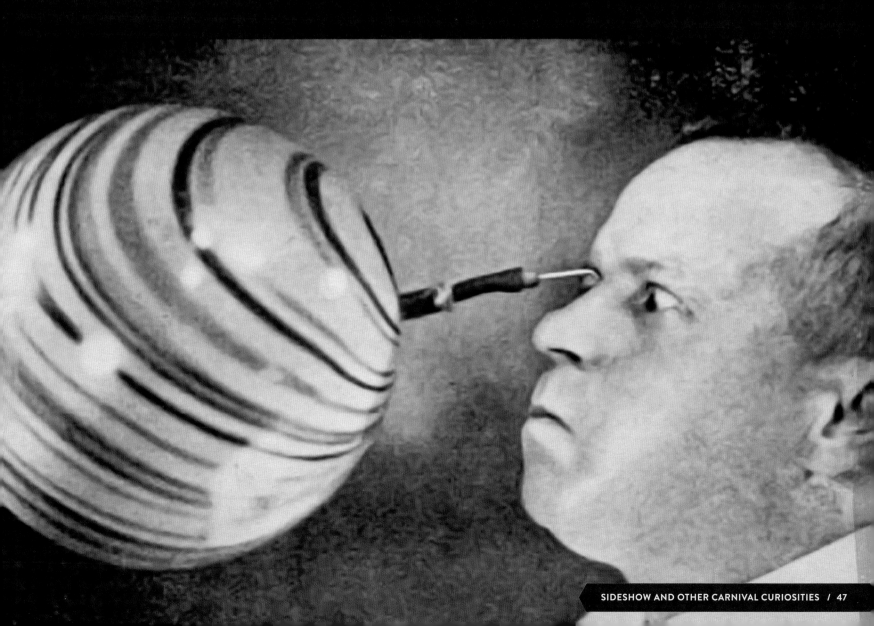

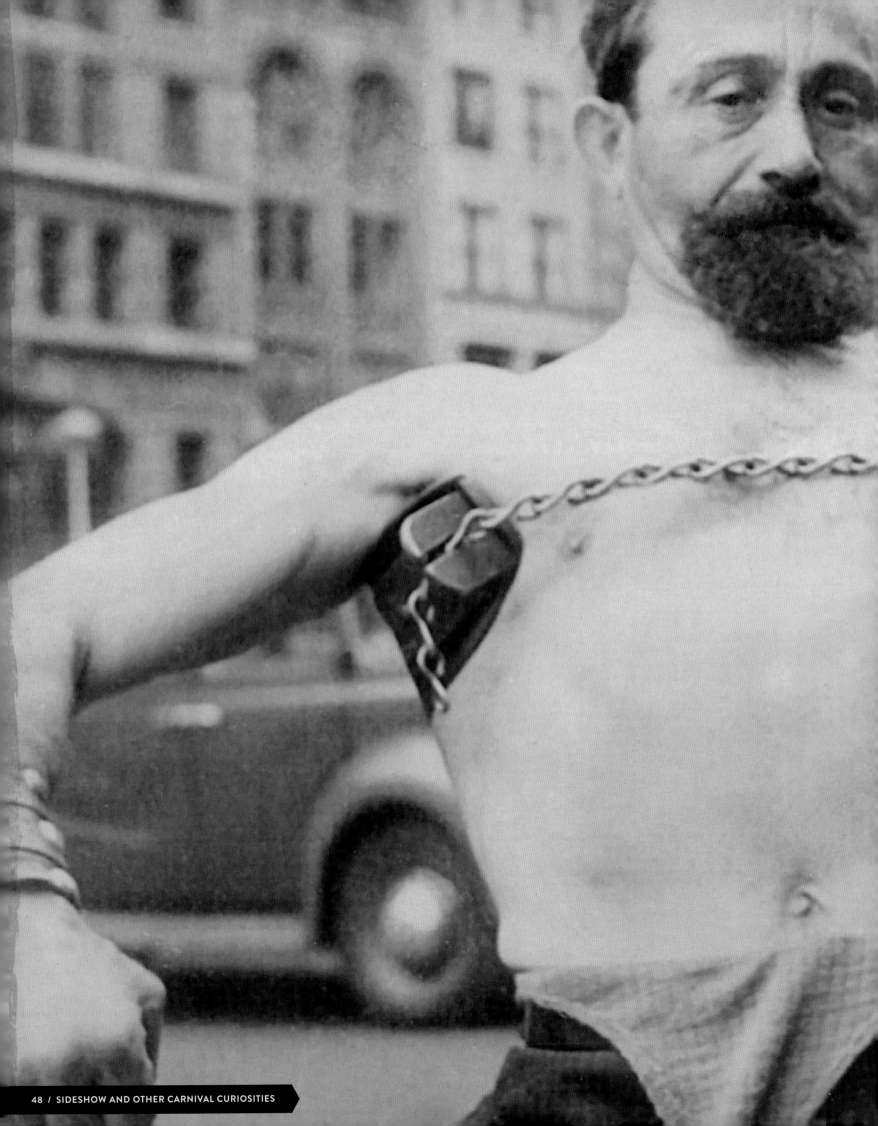

JOSEPH GREENSTEIN

STAGE NAME: THE MIGHTY ATOM

STAGE NAME: THE MIGHTY ATOM

So many remarkable feats of strength have graced the sideshow annals over the years, but no strongman had as much of an impact as Joseph "The Mighty Atom" Greenstein.

JOSEPH GREENSTEIN

Joseph Greenstein was born premature in Poland in 1893 and was reportedly a sickly child. One day he visited a touring circus, where a Russian wrestler and circus strongman noticed something in the young boy, and helped transform him from small and weak into a pocket powerhouse wrestler.

The young Greenstein even accompanied the Russian wrestler on tour to learn the art of the strongman. He visited Asia and studied martial arts, becoming interested in developing the mind as well as the body. He would credit the mental control that he learned in the Far East as being the true source of his great strength. Greenstein later arrived in the United States, finding work in the Texas oil fields.

While living in Houston, his remarkable physical capabilities made the news after a bizarre accident in which he was shot in the head by a friend's pistol. Luckily, his skull was so strong that the bullet was flattened and did not penetrate the bone. Later Greenstein bought a gas station, where he got his big break. It's said that Houdini pulled up with a flat tire one day, and after Greenstein changed it for a new one with his bare hands, the legendary magician suggested that he might have a future in show business.

Standing only 5 ft 4 in (1.6 m) and weighing around 150 lb (68 kg), Joseph Greenstein became The Mighty Atom, and he moved to the Bronx in New York City, where he mastered creative feats of strength that belied his diminutive stature. He could bend iron bars using his teeth, bite nails and steel chains in half, and tie horseshoes in knots. Greenstein also became something of a local hero after singlehandedly fighting off a gang of Nazis who were terrorizing his neighborhood.

Greenstein wowed audiences at Atlantic City and Coney Island and regularly appeared in Ripley's Believe It or Not! During each performance he would send one of his children into the audience to sell a special tonic that he claimed was the secret to his strength. In 1928, he prevented a plane that was tied to his hair from taking off at Buffalo Airport, New York.

In 1934, he had a rare accident, breaking a rib during a performance in New York City. He had bitten a nail in two and bent an iron bar with his hair, and then while attempting to lift a 100-lb (45-kg) dumbbell over his head, the strain proved too much and he broke a rib. When the ambulance arrived he declined a ride, declaring instead that would pull the vehicle to the hospital with his hair.

Other Mighty Atom feats included lying on a bed of nails with the added weight of 17 band members and their instruments on top of him, pulling a 32-ton truck, and inviting people to try and bend iron bars over his nose.

But perhaps the most remarkable aspect of his story is not the feats of strength themselves, but how long he was able to perform them. At an age when other strongmen would have long since retired from the iron game, The Mighty Atom was still bending iron bars and breaking chains with his chest.

In 1977, at the age of 83, he performed as part of a martial arts exhibition at Madison Square Garden. He died that same year, demonstrating his powers to the end. He had 10 children, and his son Mike also became a strongman, certainly inheriting his father's longevity—in 2014 he appeared on TV pulling a car with his teeth in his early 90s. Greenstein is thought to have been the inspiration for the DC Comics character Atom, who first appeared in 1940.

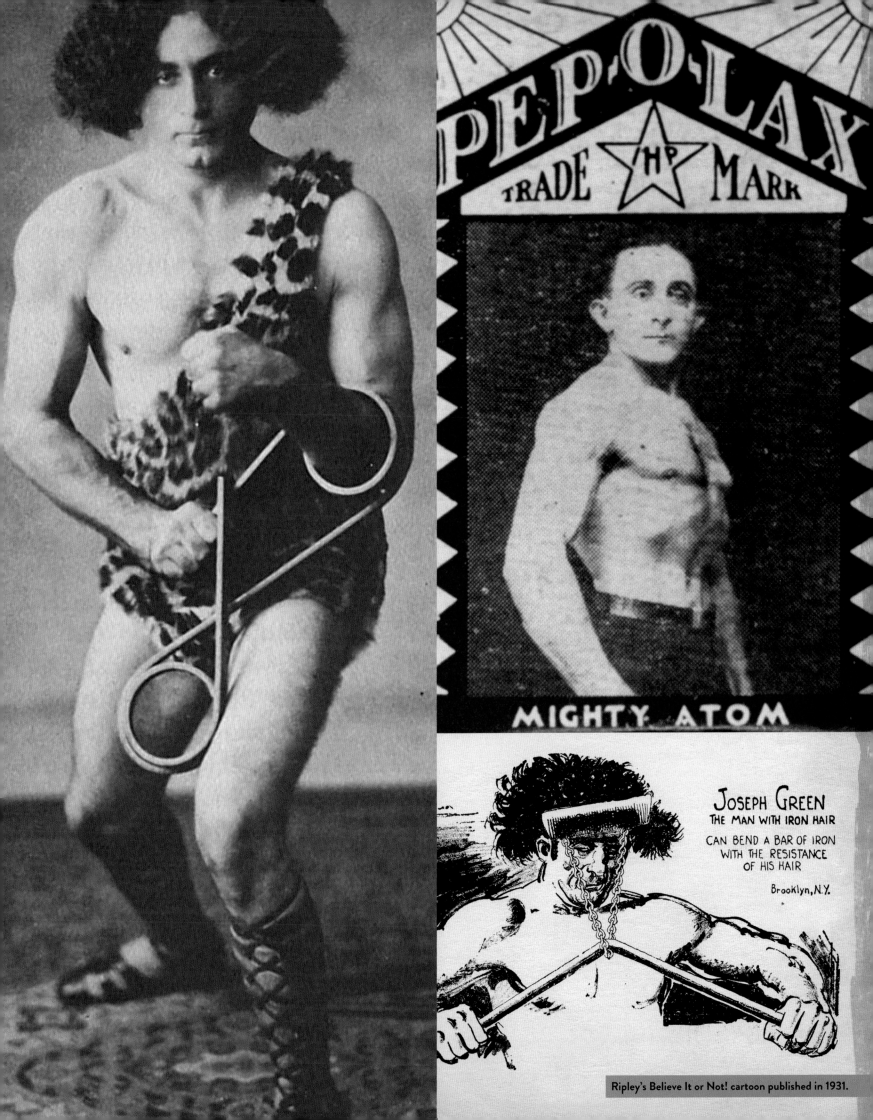

PEP·O·LAX
TRADE HP MARK

MIGHTY ATOM

JOSEPH GREEN
THE MAN WITH IRON HAIR

CAN BEND A BAR OF IRON
WITH THE RESISTANCE
OF HIS HAIR

Brooklyn, N.Y.

Ripley's Believe It or Not! cartoon published in 1931.

JOICE HETH

Joice Heth (c. 1756–1836) was an African American slave exhibited by P. T. Barnum as the 161-year-old wet nurse of President George Washington, beginning August 10, 1835.

While the details of Heth's early life evade historians to this day, she existed at the center of one of the most salacious and cruel scams in sideshow history. By 1835, Heth was owned by John S. Bowling and exhibited unsuccessfully in Louisville, Kentucky, before being sold to promoters R. W. Lindsey and Coley Bartram.

Lindsey first introduced Heth's backstory as the nanny of the infant George Washington. He also invented her astronomical age claims. But the promoters found little success promoting her. By the time she came to Barnum, she was almost completely paralyzed and blind. But she could still talk and had limited mobility in her right arm.

Besides these ailments associated with old age, she had deep-set wrinkles and fingernails resembling talons. These lent some visual credence to her advanced age claims. To further support this story, some believe Barnum forcibly removed the elderly woman's teeth, resulting in a toothless visage that helped convince sideshow visitors of her age.

During a seven-month-long tour, she traveled the country relating anecdotes about "little George" and singing hymns. According to some accounts, she raked in $1,500 per week, cementing Barnum's career in show business. After her death in New York City on February 19, 1836, Barnum permitted a public autopsy to be performed to determine her age. Fifteen hundred spectators turned out for the event. Barnum charged 50 cents apiece to attend, turning Heth's death into another money-making occasion.

Dr. David L. Rogers performed the autopsy in New York's City Saloon. His conclusion? Barnum's claims of advanced age were no more than a hoax. In reality, Heth was about 80 years old. Barnum's career was both launched and hindered by the strange case of Joice Heth. His critics often invoked the "Heth hoax" to embarrass him publicly, and as a staunch abolitionist in later life, he felt remorse for having purchased a human being early in his career.

161 YEARS OLD

THE GREATEST
Natural & National
CURIOSITY
IN THE WORLD.

JOICE HETH

Nurse to GEN. GEORGE WASHINGTON, (the Father of our Country,)
WILL BE SEEN AT

Barnum's Hotel, Bridgeport,

On FRIDAY, and SATURDAY, the 11th. & 12th days
of December, DAY and EVENING.

JOICE HETH is unquestionably the most astonishing and interesting curiosity in the World! She was the slave of Augustine Washington, (the father of Gen. Washington,) and was the first person who put clothes on the unconscious infant, who, in after days, led our heroic fathers on to glory, to victory, and freedom. To use her own language when speaking of the illustrious Father of his Country, "she raised him." JOICE HETH was born in the year 1674, and has, consequently, now arrived at the astonishing

AGE OF 161 YEARS.

She Weighs but FORTY-SIX POUNDS, and yet is very cheerful and interesting. She retains her faculties in an unparalleled degree, converses freely, sings numerous hymns, relates many interesting anecdotes of *the boy* Washington, and often laughs heartily at her own remarks, or those of the spectators. Her health is perfectly good, and her appearance very neat. She is a baptist and takes great pleasure in conversing with ministers and religious persons. The appearance of this marvellous relic of antiquity strikes the beholder with amazement, and convinces him that his eyes are resting on the oldest specimen of mortality they ever before beheld. Original, authentic, and indisputable documents accompanying her prove, however astonishing the fact may appear, that JOICE HETH is in every respect the person she is represented.

The most eminent physicians and intelligent men in Cincinnatti, Philadelphia, New-York, Boston, and other places, have examined this *living skeleton* and the documents accompanying her, and all, *invariably,* pronounce her to be, as represented, 161 *years of age!*

A female is in continual attendance, and will give every attention to the ladies who visit this relic of by-gone ages.

She has been visited in Philadelphia, New-York, Boston, &c., by more than TWENTY THOUSAND Ladies and Gentlemen, within the last three months.

Hours of Exhibition, from 9 A. M. to 1 P. M. and from 3 to 5, and 6½ to 10 P. M.

ADMITTANCE 25 Cents, CHILDREN HALF-PRICE.

Printed by J. BOOTH & SON, 147, Fulton-st N. Y.

HANNAH PERKINS AND JOHN BATTERSBY

BILLED AS: THE FAT LADY AND HER LIVING SKELETON HUSBAND

Billed as the heaviest lady in America, Hannah Perkins Battersby (1836–1889) stood in stark contrast to her husband, John Battersby (c. 1831–1897), a 50-lb (22.7-kg) thin man, yet their love story was one for the ages.

They met while working for Barnum's American Museum, where Hannah was already an established star. Unlike other contemporary fat ladies who spent inordinate amounts of time eating to bulk up, Hannah was a naturally large woman. She stood more than 6 ft (1.8 m) tall, weighed 714 lb (323.8 kg) by her mid-20s, and measured 3 ft (0.9 m) wide across her shoulders.

While some circus and sideshow couples used the hint of a relationship to generate publicity, by all accounts, Hannah and John were devoted to each other. In 1859, they welcomed a daughter named Rachel into the world. Stories also circulated about the couple's romance. Some reported that Hannah cradled John in her arms like a baby when he was sick. Others said that she rescued him from Barnum's museum fire by carrying him out of the building on her back.

By 1873, John retired from circus life as the result of a spinal injury that confined him to a wheelchair. Out of the limelight, his weight skyrocketed to 100 lb (45.3 kg). Hannah continued to perform, sending money to John and Rachel, who made a permanent home in Philadelphia.

Hannah died in 1889 from an infection sustained after falling off a stage in New Bedford, Massachusetts. According to sources, John guarded her 7-ft-wide (2.1-m) casket jealously, refusing to allow reporters or photographers near her body. After her funeral, John and Rachel relocated to the Midwest, far from the sideshow crowds.

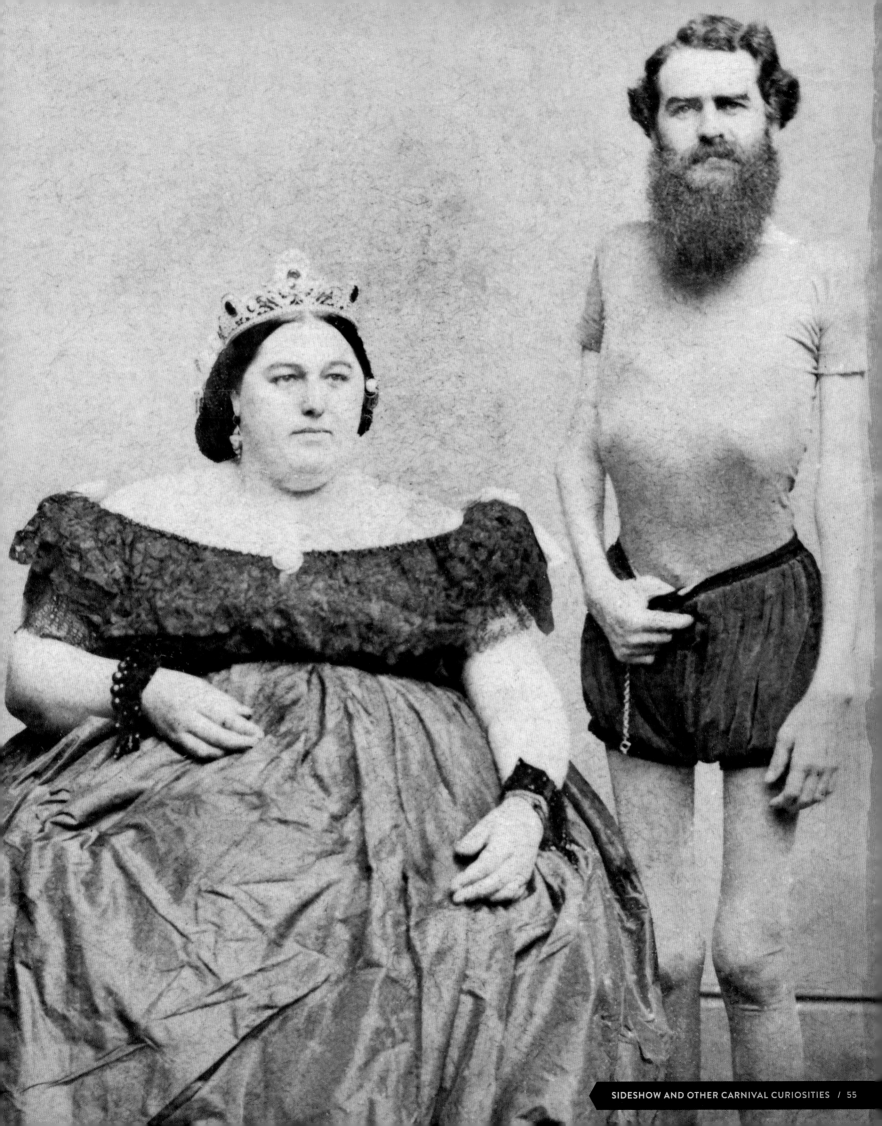

LIP PLATE TRIBE

BILLED AS: UBANGI SAVAGES

In the 1930s, the "Ubangi Savages" arrived in the United States and, after being exhibited at the Paris Zoo and in Rio de Janeiro, joined the Ringling Bros. Congress of Freaks as exotic "Duck-Billed Savages."

Wearing short, colorful skirts and no top (causing quite the sensation), the women entertained sideshow goers by sporting large wooden plates inside their lips, which were sometimes stretched up to 9 in (22.9 cm), as was customary. The women would also be paraded around the big-top arena while the band played overtly "jungle" sounding music. A "professor" (falsely) explained to the crowds that the mutilation of their lips made them unattractive to marauding kidnappers and pirates, and was thus now considered a mark of beauty. Show posters marketed the tribespeople as being "from Africa's darkest continent" and "with mouths and lips as large as those of full-grown crocodiles."

In reality, the Congolese women and their husbands were not from the Ubangi tribe. In fact, the tribe didn't exist at all. Press agent Roland Butler chose the name for its exotic sound after seeing it on a map of Africa—"Ubangi" as in the Ubangi River, part of the Congo River in central Africa. There are a few tribes in Africa that begin the lip-stretching process at the age of six, with girls gradually inserting larger disks as they grow up. Believe it or not, the term *Ubangi*, meaning "African women with lip plates," is still listed in the Merriam-Webster dictionary.

Unfortunately, the performers' French manager Eugene Bergonier was found stealing their $1,500 appearance fee, while they were left to keep the proceeds from selling their postcards. One account says the relationship between them became so contentious that the women created a doll of Bergonier and tortured it, while Bergonier took to carrying a revolver. When Bergonier died, the tribespeople were finally able to make it back to the Congo— at John Ringling's expense—and other less problematic "Ubangi Savages" were imported.

Robert Ripley meeting a lip plate tribeswoman.

RINGLING BROS
AND
BARNUM & BAILEY
PRESENT
FROM AFRICA'S DARKEST DEPTHS
TRIBE OF GENUINE
UBANGI SAVAGES
WITH MOUTHS AND LIPS AS LARGE AS
THOSE OF FULL-GROWN CROCO

RINGLING BROS and BARNUM & BAILEY
Greatest Educational Feature of All Time!
NEW TO CIVILIZATION!!!
From Africa's Darkest Depths!
TRIBE OF GENUINE
UBANGI SAVAGES
WITH MOUTHS AND LIPS AS LARGE AS

ROBERT WADLOW

KNOWN AS: THE ALTON GIANT

Robert Wadlow, born February 22, 1918, in Alton, Illinois, was a normal-sized baby, but by the time he was eight years old, he was taller than his father, who stood almost 6 ft (1.8 m) tall.

ROBERT WADLOW

He was so big that his school had to make a custom desk to fit his legs, and at 13, Wadlow was a 7 ft 4 in (2.2 m) tall Boy Scout. At his tallest, the "Alton Giant" was 8 ft 11 in (2.72 m). (The tallest man alive today, Sultan Kösen of Turkey, is a full 8 in [20.3 cm] shorter.) Word of the young "Illinois Giant" soon spread, and he embarked on a tour of America with his father, visiting 800 towns. When the pair traveled by car, Wadlow would sit in the back with the front passenger seat removed to make room for his legs. His feet were so big—thought to be the largest ever—that he required shoes almost 20 in (50 cm) long, a U.S. size 37AA, costing as much as an average month's salary at the time.

The Alton Giant turned down various offers to appear in circus sideshows, which often featured much smaller "giants" of the time, but in 1936 he agreed to sign up with the famous Ringling Bros. Circus on the condition that he appear not in the sideshow but the main circus arena. He would make short, dignified cameo roles at famous venues such as Madison Square Garden, always wearing a smart suit tailored for his enormous frame.

Wadlow's great height stemmed from an overactive pituitary gland that produced an abnormal amount of growth hormone. This meant that he never stopped growing, and at his heaviest he weighed almost 500 lb (227 kg). Wadlow's size and busy schedule took a toll on his health, and as a 21-year-old he already had braces on his legs and walked with the aid of a cane. One year later, in 1940, he died from an infection caused by blisters from his leg braces. Wadlow died one month after being measured at almost 9 ft (2.7 m) high, the tallest person to have ever lived.

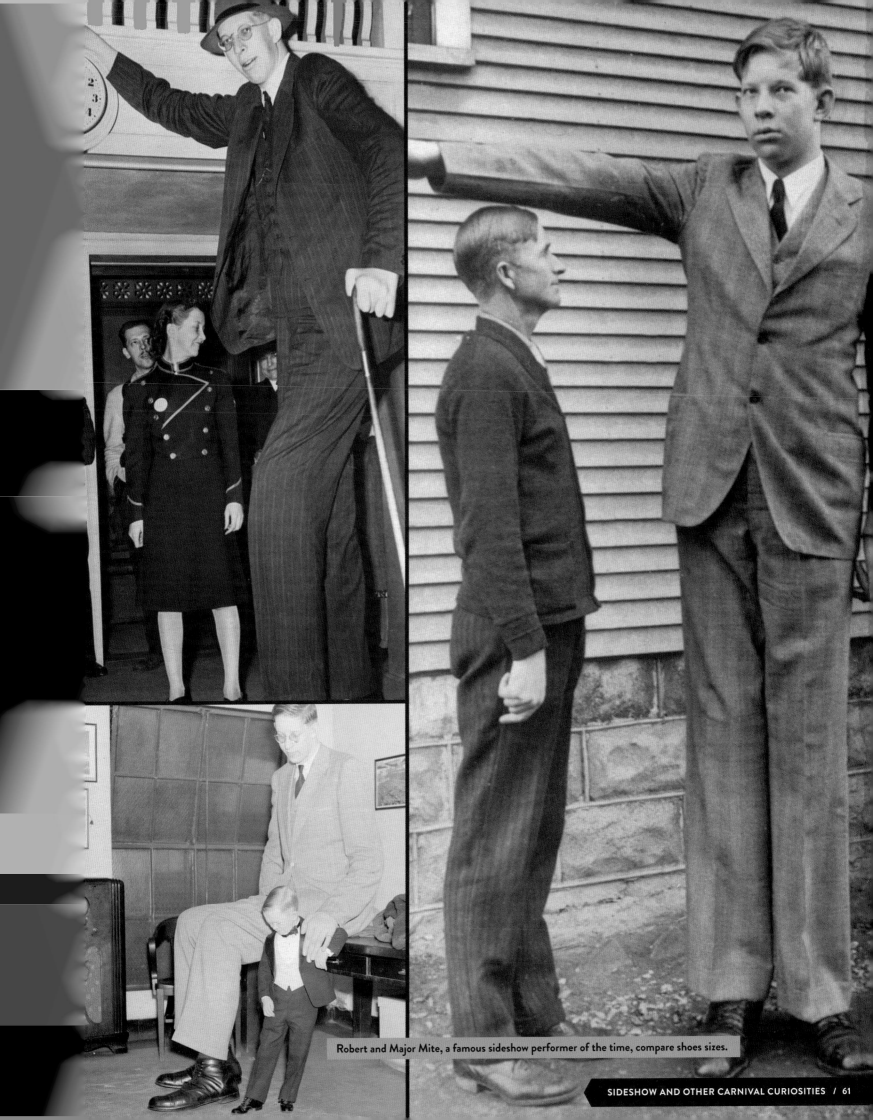

Robert and Major Mite, a famous sideshow performer of the time, compare shoes sizes.

"LOOK AT LIFE" PRESENTS BIG— BABY BERTHA AND SLIM JIM

"THE MRS." BIG BERTHA 540 LBS.

"THE MR." SLIM JIM 68 LBS.

"BELIEVE IT OR NOT"

New York World's Fair Museum presents

"BELIEVE IT OR NO[T]"

WEIGHT 540 LBS.

Subjects as cartooned by ROBT. L RIPLEY

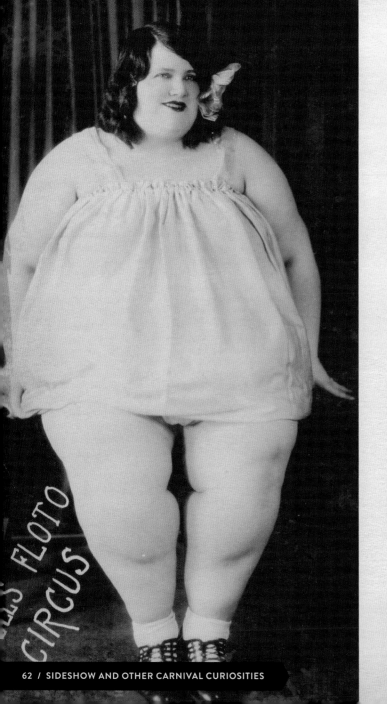

SELLS FLOTO CIRCUS

BERTHA CURTIS

BILLED AS: BIG BERTHA; BIG BABY BERTHA

"Big Baby Bertha," a 540-lb (244.9-kg) fat lady, headlined at the New York World's Fair Museum from 1939 to 1940 and was immortalized in illustrated posters by Robert Ripley.

Across the United States and Europe, the girth and jiggle of obese sideshow performers drew crowds to circuses, dime museums, and carnivals alike. Renowned among the fat folks was Bertha Curtis, or "Big Baby Bertha." She often appeared alongside her awkwardly mismatched husband "Slim Jim" Curtis. Slim Jim stood 6 ft (1.8 m) tall and fluctuated between 68 and 89 lb (31 to 40 kg).

Through "thick and thin," Bertha and Jim entertained curious crowds who came to watch them dance and sing. By 1943, they appeared with other performers in York, Pennsylvania, at the midway billed as the "Skeleton Dude" and his "Congress of Fat Folks." That same year, Jim and Bertha appeared as the "strangest married couple" in Ray Marsh Brydon's International Congress of Oddities alongside famous sideshow acts like Grace McDaniels, the "Mule-Faced Woman."

LION MOTORDROME

From the 1930s through the 1960s, the lion drome circuit pitted stunt riders against lions in a "Race for Life," where speed and power ruled.

Stunt riders in the 1930s risked life and limb in circular board racing tracks known as motordromes, wowing crowds with their daring. Yet, the popularity of their acts hinged on shock and awe. This meant constantly upping the ante to draw larger crowds.

In the 1930s, the introduction of live lions to motordomes did the trick. Audiences marveled as the stunt drivers raced around the tracks while lions swatted at them and attempted to tackle them. But when these stunts grew tiresome, it was time for another round of re-invention.

Riders started driving trained lions around in sidecars, tackling the almost perpendicular walls of the motordome at 80 mph (129 kmph). Of course, the feat wasn't without its risks. Marjorie Kemp, a seasoned lion drome rider, got mauled four separate times and spent more than a year in the hospital after her last attack in 1940.

CATHERINE BRUMBACH

STAGE NAME: SANDWINA

BILLED AS: QUEEN OF STRENGTH AND BEAUTY

The daughter of a famed German circus family, Sandwina wowed audiences with her feats of strength, which included wrestling men and lifting her husband over her head with one hand.

Catherine "Katie" Brumbach (1884–1952) was born to a family of Bavarian circus performers who toured Europe regularly. Her father, Philippe, stood 6 ft 6 in (1.9 m) tall, weighed 260 lb (117.9 kg), and had a chest that measured 56 in (142.2 cm) across. Her mother, Johanna, was a strong woman in her own right who shocked audiences with her feats of strength and 15-in (38.1-cm) biceps.

Of their 15 children, only a few inherited the couple's sturdy build and strong constitutions. While Catherine may not have been the strongest of them, she made up for this in natural beauty and a perfectly proportioned physique. By the age of two, Catherine could do handstands on her father's hands. Trained in gymnastics, she added weightlifting to her regimen as she matured.

By 16, the tall beauty added a new trick to her routine. Philippe offered a 100-German-mark prize to any man who could successfully beat her at wrestling, yet each time a new gentleman came onstage, she quickly subdued him.

One fateful evening, a 5 ft 6 in (1.7 m) acrobat named Max Heymann (who was 19 years old) decided to take her up on the offer. Catherine won the match, but Heymann stole her heart. Within two years, they married, and he became a permanent part of the family act. To demonstrate her amazing strength, Catherine often lifted Heymann overhead using one arm. After their sons were born, she added them to the show, lifting her whole family.

After competing in a strength competition against Eugen Sandow, the most famous bodybuilder of his day, Catherine bested him by lifting 300 lb (136 kg) over her head. Sandow couldn't get the weight past his chest. To commemorate her victory, she took the stage name Sandwina. Soon, her entire troupe was known as the Sandwinas. The "Queen of Beauty and Strength" entertained audiences for years by twisting iron bars into spirals, juggling cannonballs, breaking chains with her bare hands, supporting a 1,200-lb (544.3-kg) cannonball on her shoulders, and more.

(From left to right) Moung-Phoset, his mother Maphoon, and his daughter Mah-Mé.

HAIRY FAMILY

STAGE NAME: SACRED HAIRY FAMILY OF BURMA

Several generations of "The Sacred Hairy Family of Burma," as they were known, lived and performed at the court of the King of Burma in the 19th century.

(From left to right) Maphoon, her granddaughter Mah-Mé (around age 7) standing on a chair, and her son Moung-Phoset (in his 20s) sitting on a stool.

HAIRY FAMILY

The family's story begins with the patriarch Shwe-Maong. The local chief of his district gifted him to the King of Ava, a province of Burma, when he was only 5 years old. At various points, visiting dignitaries and physicians were able to examine Shwe-Maong and converse with him. In 1826, John Crawfurd reported back that Shwe-Maong stated his parents were perfectly normal and that none of his tribesmen was hairy.

He entertained the king so well that at the age of 22, the king chose a wife for him, and Shwe-Maong fathered four children—all girls. Two children died young, and one girl inherited her mother's normal looks, while the other surviving child, named Maphoon, inherited her father's hypertrichosis (meaning her face was also entirely covered in thick hair). Shwe-Maong was later murdered by robbers, and his daughter Maphoon was brought up in the king's household.

By 1855, the 31-year-old Maphoon was married to a normal Burmese man and became the mother of two boys. The king arranged her marriage by offering a reward to any man who was willing to marry her. Of Maphoon's two boys, the elder son was normal, and her second son was hairy.

At some point, the hairy son, named Moung-Phoset, married one of the maids of honor at the court, just like his grandfather did, although this time his wife freely chose him. The couple had several children, including a daughter named Mah-Mé with the same hairy condition.

In 1885, the Third Burmese War broke out, and the revolution drove the family from the palace. Italian officer Captain Paperno rescued them and was so amazed by their appearance that he suggested they travel to Europe to make their fortune as living exhibits. Sadly, Moung-Phoset's daughter Mah-Mé died at the age of 18 before the family left for Europe. Paperno acted as their manager, and in 1886, Maphoon, her son Moung-Phoset, and the rest of the family, all covered in hair, appeared in London to the great interest of the public.

They later traveled to Paris, France, and in the 1890s found fame in the U.S. sideshow of legendary showman P.T. Barnum, where they performed for one year as "Unearthly Beings," including an appearance at Madison Square Garden in New York City. Following their short stint in the United States, the family disappeared, and the fate of Maphoon and her son Moung-Phoset is a mystery. To this day, the hairy family of Burma is the only example of a four-generation pedigree of congenital hypertrichosis.

Congenital hypertrichosis is an extremely rare condition that affects just a tiny fraction of the population. There have been only about 50 cases ever recorded, and only a handful of people on the planet are currently living with the disorder. Often known as "Werewolf Syndrome," hypertrichosis emerges in childhood and causes thick, long hair to grow all over the face, and in some cases the entire body, leaving only the palms of the hands and the soles of the feet hairless. It is a hereditary disease, meaning it is passed through generations of the same family from

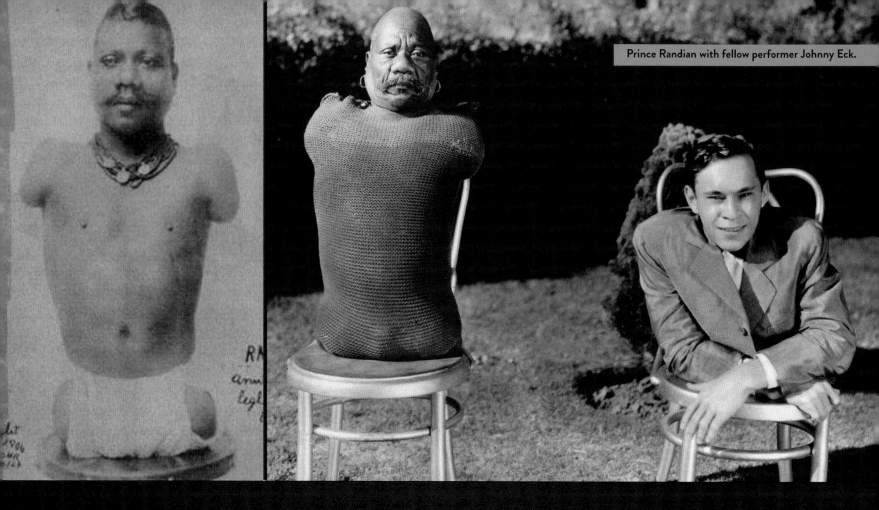

Prince Randian with fellow performer Johnny Eck.

PRINCE RANDIAN

STAGE NAME: THE LIVING TORSO; THE SNAKE MAN; THE HUMAN CATERPILLAR

Born with tetra-amelia syndrome, Prince Randian (1871–1934) turned this tragedy into a money-making triumph as a famous limbless performer in the 19th and 20th centuries.

Prince Randian was born in Demerara, British Guyana. A gifted man, he could speak French, German, Hindi, and English with ease and was a self-avowed Hindu. Brought to the United States by P. T. Barnum in 1889 at the age of 18, Prince Randian wowed crowds with his ability to perform a variety of mundane tasks despite being limbless. This included rolling a cigarette using nothing more than his lips.

To enhance the snake-like appearance of his limbless

his shoulders and hips. Besides rolling cigarettes, he also painted and wrote, holding the brush or stylus between his lips. He could even shave his face by securing a razor in a wooden block. Best of all, each of these implements was kept in a wooden box that he locked himself and claimed to have built and painted.

Along with Pip and Flip and the Hilton Sisters, Prince Randian appeared in *Freaks* (1932), where he is shown lighting a cigarette with a match despite being armless, handless, and fingerless.

Despite his career on the freak-show circuit, Prince Randian enjoyed a relatively normal home life. Married to Princess Sarah, a Hindu woman born circa

WAIN ESPER PRESENTS

FREAKS

LOUELLA PA

FOR PURE SENSATIONAL SH

FLEA CIRCUS

Flea circuses enjoyed immense popularity between the 1830s and 1960s, and represented a combination of iron-clad chutzpah, flamboyant showmanship, and authentic craftsmanship.

Roloff's Floh-Circus

WILH. ROLOFF

THE

CURIOUS AND AMUSING

EXHIBITION

OF THE

EDUCATED FLEAS.

WITH

NOTES, OBSERVATIONS AND INTERESTING
ANECDOTES,

BY L. BERTOLOTTO,

THE ORIGINAL INVENTOR.

FIFTH EDITION. REVISED.

PRICE, TWENTY-FIVE CENTS.

FLEA CIRCUS

From the mid-19th to mid-20th centuries, no circus was complete without a tent dedicated to fleas. Flea circuses included the rapid narration of a "professor," a title given to all flea-circus ringmasters.

In the beginning, flea circuses focused on craftsmanship. Displayed as miniature objects, visitors marveled at their handiwork. But an enterprising Italian showman changed all of that.

Louis Bertolotto became the impresario of the flea-circus world after taking his shows to the next level. He narrated the imaginary happenings in the ring, delighting audiences with his fleas' microscopic antics. In the process, he launched a veritable phenomenon.

Fleas are not organisms known for their dramatic flair. But the human variant has strong back legs. This made them excellent jumpers and the perfect creatures to excite crowds through dynamic bursts of energy. And because they fed on human blood, keeping them alive proved easy. All the professor had to do was roll up a sleeve and let them feast.

Soon, innovative professors started attaching fleas to circus props. They also wove yarn around their flea-training regimens. Some fleas walked tightropes. Others were painstakingly harnessed to miniature chariots and ran races. Many professors migrated from other trades such as jewelry or watchmaking. This education equipped them with the know-how to craft miniature props.

By the 1950s, flea circuses nosedived in popularity. Concerns about animal cruelty hampered them, as did a new awareness of the importance of basic hygiene. Almost overnight, flea-circus performers fell prey to vacuums and cleanliness.

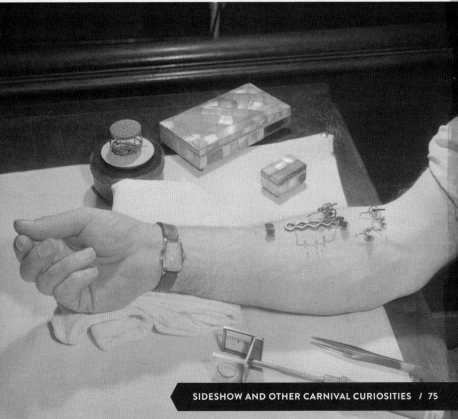

JASON BLACK

BILLED AS: BLACK SCORPION

Performer Jason Black was born with the rare medical condition ectrodactyly (or lobster claw syndrome), which has left him with only two large pincerlike fingers, a thumb on each hand, and three toes on each foot.

"THE FREAKSHOW IS THERE TO AFFECT."
—JASON BLACK

JASON BLACK

Black has used his deformity to his advantage by reinventing himself as the Black Scorpion and touring the United States as a dynamic magician and sideshow performer who swallows balloons, escapes from handcuffs, and walks on broken glass.

In addition to working for more than 15 years at an Austin, Texas, news station, he is the creative director, writer, and performer with the 999 Eyes Freakshow. The sideshow features body-modified performers and vaudeville-style artists such as sword swallowers and human pincushions, as well as artists with genetic anomalies such as Black himself.

Black first got into performing after meeting Joe Hermann (aka The Amazing Mr. Lifto) at a friend's wedding. Black says, "He was the first person who'd ever made me feel good about my hands and feet. Before I met Joe I really didn't think of them as a gift—more as that little something that keeps me from living a normal life." Since he

started touring with 999 Eyes, he has found that his fellow performers think his hands and feet are simply awesome.

Wearing his trademark multicolored bandit mask and proudly displaying his claws, the Black Scorpion aims to change people's perceptions by making them realize that "freaks" are no different from any of the members of the audience. Black's signature act is what he dubs "Hammer Hands": while wearing gloves, he smashes a hammer on his fingers but then shocks the audience by removing the gloves and revealing his split hands.

He's gone on to perform at Coney Island and at the Museum of Weird in Austin, Texas. In 2014, Black was a consultant for actor Evan Peters's character on the fourth season of *American Horror Story: Freak Show*. Recently, Black started selling castings of his hands to help cover medical and dental bills, as his ectrodactyly has gradually deteriorated his health.

THE IGORROTE VILLAGE

In 1905, one of the most popular attractions at Coney Island was the Igorrote Village.

Feeding off the fear and amazement evoked by the unknown, 50 Filipino tribesmen, women, and children lived in a replica village and presented a sensationalized version of their customs. They would dance barefoot, wearing nothing but loincloths, and—as head hunting was not an option—slaughter dogs brought from the pound in front of the crowd and then cook the meat in a large pot.

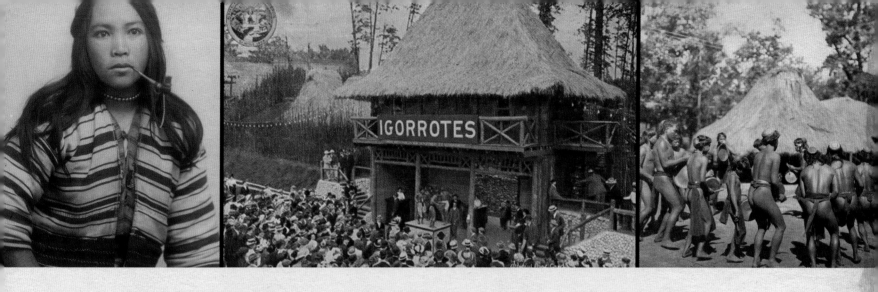

THE IGORROTE VILLAGE

The tribespeople hailed from the region of Bontoc in the Philippines, a remote portion of the country that was torn apart by the Spanish-American War. The initial idea to bring 50 tribesmen to the states for exhibition was formulated by showman Truman Hunt, a former medical doctor who stayed in the Philippines after the war ended and became a lieutenant governor of Bontoc. He knew the tribe well, offering them $15 a month to leave their family and friends for a year to be put on display in America. They took the deal.

Competition heated up when Richard Schneidewind, another Spanish-American War veteran, arrived in America with his own troupe of Filipino Igorrotes. There was a marked difference between how each showman treated his tribe—Hunt treated them like a commodity, while Schneidewind treated them like family, going so much as to invite them to his home to have dinner with his family.

Schneidewind's tribe exhibited at the 1905 Lewis and Clark Centennial Exposition in Portland, Oregon, and then wowed crowds at Chutes Park in Los Angeles. Hunt, on the other hand, split up his tribespeople, desperately trying to increase profits. The rivalry was so intense they would try to undermine each other's exhibitions.

Unfortunately, Hunt mistreated the tribespeople in his care. Schneidewind eventually reported to a government agency that Hunt's village was in terrible condition and that 18 people were living in three small tents in the mud. Hunt went on the run with a few tribespeople after he caught wind that government investigators were on their way. A manhunt ensued, and Hunt was eventually arrested and tried.

Schneidewind then had a monopoly on the Bontoc Igorrotes in showbusiness. Sadly, after a few years of traveling and a disastrous stint on the European circuit, where the showman could no longer afford to pay the tribespeople and living conditions were so bad that tribe members were dying, the U.S. government intervened, sending the Igorrotes back to Manila.

In 1914, the Philippine Assembly passed legislation banning the exhibition of Filipino tribespeople abroad, an amendment to the Anti-Slavery Act.

DAGMAR ROTHMAN

STAGE NAME: THE GREAT WALDO

BILLED AS: THE REGURGITATING GEEK; THE HUMAN OSTRICH

Born in Germany, Dagmar Rothman, or The Great Waldo, specialized in bizarre acts of regurgitation. He could put a real live mouse in his mouth, swallow it, and open his mouth to show the audience that it really had been swallowed. Then he would somehow bring the creature up from his stomach in one piece, and let it crawl out of his mouth, totally unharmed.

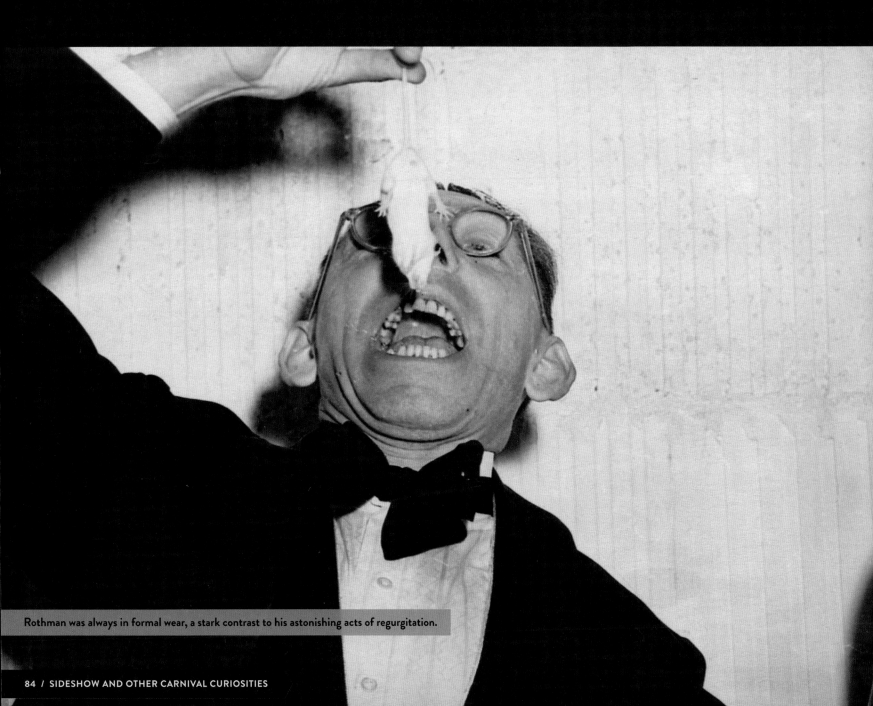

Rothman was always in formal wear, a stark contrast to his astonishing acts of regurgitation.

While the mouse was swallowed, Rothman would proceed to light and smoke a cigarette, claiming that the smoke helped pacify the rodent.

Rothman was also known as "The Regurgitating Geek." In sideshow lingo, a "geek" was someone who would swallow bizarre objects for entertainment. Rothman differentiated himself by bringing back up what he had already swallowed.

He would swallow and bring up various items belonging to audience members, including keys, coins, and watches—inviting its owner to listen to the timepiece ticking in his stomach. He even swallowed fish, taking care to swallow plenty of water so that they didn't suffocate. He was so adept at controlling his throat and stomach muscles that he could swallow different colored balls, and regurgitate them in whichever order he liked. Perhaps The Great Waldo's most perplexing trick was to swallow a locked padlock, then a key, and regurgitate the padlock—unlocked.

Rothman performed around Germany and Austria in the 1930s, escaping to Switzerland when Hitler invaded Austria in 1938. An American talent agent saw his act one night and persuaded him to take his unique ability across the Atlantic. It was in the United States where Rothman found fame, performing at Ripley's Odditoriums and the Ringling Bros. Circus sideshows.

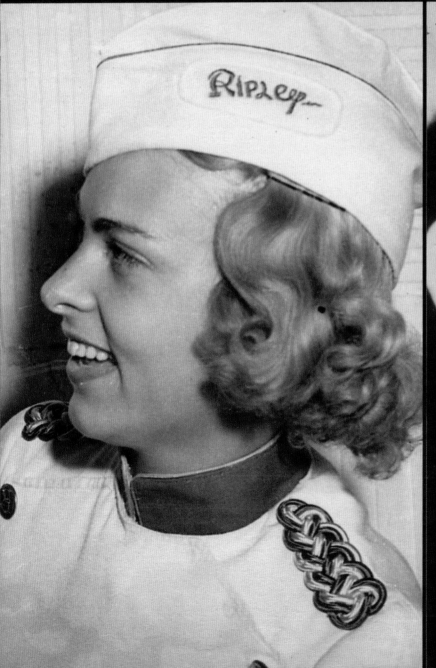

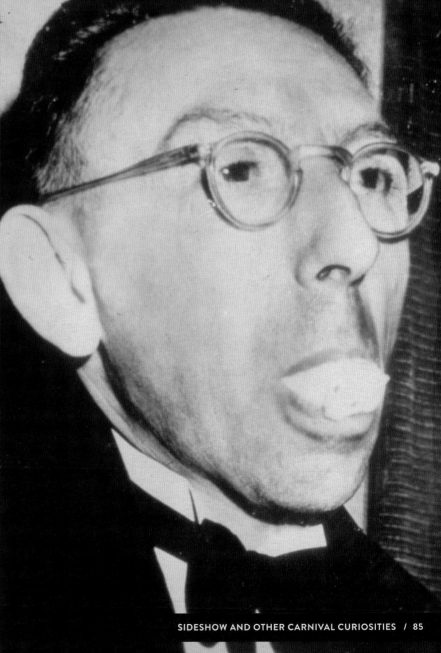

DWAIN ESPER PRESENTS

FREAKS

LOUELLA PARSONS *SAYS—*
FOR PURE SENSATIONALISM 'FREAKS' TOPS ANY PICTURE
YET PRODUCED. IT'S MORE FANTASTIC AND GROTESQUE
THAN ANY SHOCKER EVER WRITTEN

EXCLUSIVE FOREIGN DISTRIBUTION CONTROLLED BY
EXCELSIOR PICT. CORP.
NEW YORK 19, U.S.A.

SCHLITZIE

BILLED AS: MAGGIE, THE LAST OF THE AZTEC CHILDREN

Not much is known about this iconic sideshow performer's early life. Some contend that Schlitzie was born Simon Metz in 1901 in the Bronx, New York, but one thing is known for sure: Schlitzie was born with the neurodevelopmental disorder microcephaly.

Along with a diminutive stature (he was barely 4 ft [1.2 m] tall), he exhibited a small brain and a skull that pointed slightly, which is where the common term "pinhead" derived. With his severe mental disability, Schlitzie never developed cognitively past three or four years of age, but his childlike innocence and smiling, happy demeanor are well documented.

Although Schlitzie was not the only pinhead in the sideshow world, he was certainly the most lovable and famous. Spending years on the circus circuit with the likes of Ringling Bros. and Barnum & Bailey, he performed as a woman, nearly always wearing a dress—a practical attire choice because of his incontinence, which required him to use diapers. Like many other pinheads of the time, he was billed as "The Last of the Aztec Children," a reference to when mysterious early humans and specifically Mesoamerican cultures would reshape their skulls.

He made the jump to films with 1928's *The Sideshow*, but it was Tod Browning's *Freaks* in 1932 that cemented Schlitzie in pop-culture history. Sometime in the late 1930s, chimpanzee trainer George Surtees became his legal guardian, but when he died in the early 1960s, his daughter placed Schlitzie in a mental institution in Los Angeles.

It wasn't until sword-swallower Bill Unks, who was working at the hospital in the off-season, recognized the depressed Schlitzie that he was rescued and returned to the sideshow he loved. Schlitzie never fully retired, but he did live in an apartment in downtown Los Angeles. He could be seen feeding the pigeons and ducks around a lake, where he danced and performed for passersby.

Schlitzie passed away in 1971 at the age of 70 (although he could have been older, since his birth year is unknown). He is immortalized in pop culture, as both Bill Griffith's *Zippy the Pinhead* comic strip and The Ramones song "Pinhead" are about him, and *American Horror Story: Freak Show* had a character based on the lovable sideshow performer.

JUDGE
DESMUKE
ARMLESS
KNIFE
THROWER

THROWS
10 BUTCHER KNIVES
WITHIN ONE INCH OF
HIS WIFE STANDING **7** FEET AWAY

PAUL DESMUKE

Paul Desmuke was born in April 1876 in Texas and made a name for himself as an armless knife thrower.

Born without arms, Desmuke learned to use his feet as dexterously as others use their hands, and it's said that he could play a mean fiddle. Before joining the sideshow, however, he became the Justice of the Peace for his small Texas town, and thus he earned the nickname Judge.

He eventually learned how to throw knives, using his wife Mae Dixon as the "target" in his impalement act, and signed on with the A. G. Barnes Circus and Sideshow, as well as a Wild West show. Desmuke even dabbled in acting, appearing in the silent films *The Unknown* in 1927 and *The Sideshow* in 1928.

Most famously, Desmuke performed at the Ripley's Odditoriums, including the 1933 Century of Progress Expo in Chicago.

The sideshow star lived out the rest of life in his native Texas and passed away in 1949.

SUTHERLAND SISTERS

BILLED AS: 7 WONDERS OF THE WORLD! 7 ACCOMPLISHED MUSICIANS! 7 LADIES WITH 49 FEET OF HAIR! 7 FEET OF HAIR EACH!

NEW DIM...
A SELECT FAMILY RESOR...
Horticultural Hall Buildin...
Open from 10 a....

FIRST APPEARANCE OF THE
MATCHLESS! INCOMPARABLE!
SEVEN
Sutherland Sisters
7 WONDERS OF THE WORLD!
LONG HAIRED SISTERS!
SONGSTERS!
ECCENTRIC ...IES!
...ISHED MU...S! 7
...d Educat...
OF
...ND
...

SUTHERLAND SISTERS

In the late 1800s, seven sisters from upstate New York wowed crowds with their long locks, touring the world at dime museums, P.T. Barnum's circus sideshows, and even world's fairs.

The Sutherland sisters—Sarah, Victoria, Isabella, Grace, Naomi, Dora, and Mary—came from humble beginnings, growing up on their family's turkey farm, where their mother concocted a smelly lotion to make their hair grow... and grow it did. The long-haired ladies happened to share 37 ft (11.3 m) of hair between them—a length exaggerated later in their career.

They initially began their life in show business as talented singers and musicians, but people didn't flock to see their skill so much as to see them let loose their luscious locks. This was quite a spectacle, because while long hair was fashionable in the Victorian era, any respectable woman would always keep her hair up in polite society.

The family began to market their hair more than their talents and capitalized on the patent medicine trend by selling what they called "hair fertilizer" at their shows. They claimed that it was the secret lotion that their mother had used to make their tumbling tresses grow so long, but it was actually just a mixture of alcohol, oil, and water that they had recently invented. (Their mother had already died and taken the hair growth recipe with her to the grave.)

Despite this, the concoction made them rich: along with other ointments and soaps, they netted $90,000 in sales the first year. When Naomi died in 1893, the family simply hired a replacement to keep the show on the road. The Sutherland Sisters fell out of favor when short bobbed hair became the fashion, but they still managed to make around $3 million over the course their career. The girls used the money to build a mansion on the family farm, where they lived much of the rest of their lives together, as only two of the sisters ever married.

PHINEAS GAGE

Phineas Gage should have died when an iron rod blasted through his face and out of the top of his head. Instead, he survived and became one of the most unbelievable medical stories in history, even making an appearance at P. T. Barnum's American Museum.

Gage was a foreman for a railroad company in Vermont who blasted rocks to clear space for the tracks to be laid. One day in September 1848, the 25-year-old was preparing a detonation, packing gunpowder into holes in the rock using a 43 in (110 cm) iron tamping rod. Usually Gage would wait for his assistant to lay sand over the explosives before he used the rod, but this time he didn't, and as he struck with the metal bar, the powder ignited. Instead of cracking the rock, the explosion propelled the 13 lb (6 kg) iron rod right through Gage's face and out of the top of his head with such force that it landed several dozen feet away, covered with "blood and brain."

It should surely have been a fatal injury, but instead the incident began one of the most remarkable stories in medical history. Gage was not dead—indeed, he may not have even lost consciousness—and he was able to walk away from the scene while talking to his coworkers. One account says he spat out "about half a teacupful" of his brain matter as a doctor examined him, but he was still able to tell the physician, "Here is business enough for you." Gage lost consciousness after his wound became infected, but after several months he made a miraculous recovery. All his motor functions were intact, but he was blind in the left eye, which the rod damaged on its way through his skull.

Gage's case became famous; he was even photographed with the offending iron rod and his left eye closed, but with no other visible sign of injury. Although Gage was physically able—he lived for 11 years after the accident—mentally he was not the same, or in his doctor's words, "no longer Gage," and friends reported that post-explosion Gage was irritable, angry, and untrustworthy, to the extent that he was unable to return to his old job. His memory and intelligence were the same as before, but he had lost his inhibitions and his ability to function in civilized society, impulsively indulging in the "grossest profanity."

After failing to find work on the railroads, Gage made public appearances with the offending tamping iron, even being paraded at Barnum's famous American Museum in New York City. He traveled to Chile to find a job on stagecoaches and eventually returned home to work on the family farm, where he died in 1860, aged 36. He had been suffering seizures likely linked to his brain damage. Doctors would study the injury for many years; Gage's case gave a valuable early insight into how the brain could function after serious injury, and how brain damage in different areas of the organ could affect behavior. Gage's story made such an impact on medical study that his skull—with a large hole clearly visible—and the iron rod can be seen today in the Harvard Medical School museum.

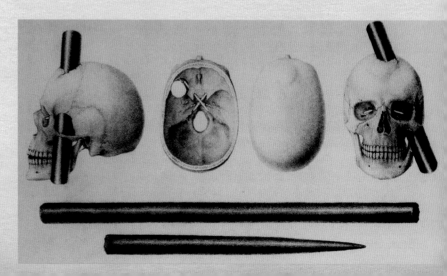

CHARLOTTE VOGEL

STAGE NAME: SUSI

BILLED AS: THE ELEPHANT SKIN GIRL

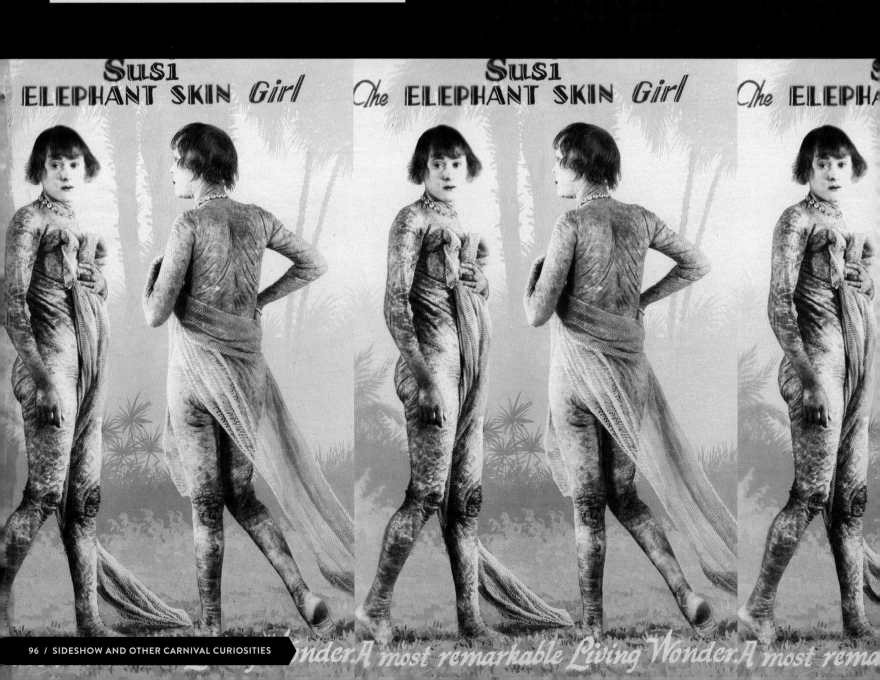

Charlotte Vogel (1900–1916) of Germany suffered from a rare and debilitating condition known as ichthyosis, which gave her skin an elephantine appearance.

Carnival sideshows often featured individuals who suffered from ichthyosis. The vast majority marketed themselves as alligator-like because of the disease's telltale scaly skin. But Charlotte's condition proved unique. It manifested aggressively in early childhood. Because of its severity, she experienced constant pain and was prone to skin infections.

Simply blinking her eyes could cause dangerous cracks in her skin, which proved vulnerable to infection. The disease robbed her of the ability to cry or sweat. During the summer, she resorted to rubbing ice on her skin to avoid overheating. Because of the elephant-like look of her thick, gray skin, she endured constant ridicule.

To improve her physical well-being and appearance, her parents started rubbing her skin with lotion and oil every day. They peeled the skin on her face nightly, too. These practices improved her appearance and comfort, revealing a clear, attractive face. This daily routine became standard practice for the rest of her life.

Charlotte first visited America in 1927 with a troupe of sideshow performers that included a bearded lady and a giantess. She and her manager eventually immigrated to the United States. She lived in an apartment on New York's west side. Throughout the 1930s, she often exhibited herself at Coney Island and Hubert's Museum on 42nd Street. In 1967, she exhibited at the Ringling show in Madison Square Garden, one of the highlights of her career.

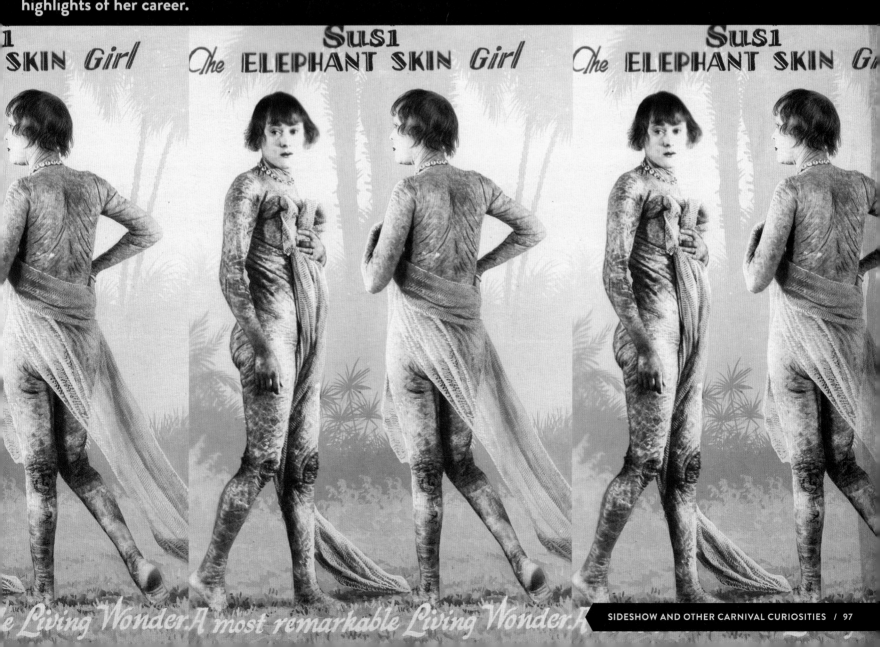

MIKE THE HEADLESS CHICKEN

STAGE NAME: MIRACLE MIKE

HOMETOWN: FRUITA, COLORADO

On September 10, 1945, farmer Lloyd Olsen was slaughtering chickens on his farm in Fruita, Colorado. He selected a five-month-old Wyandotte rooster named Mike and chopped the chicken's head off with a single axe blow. Miraculously, the chicken didn't die.

Not only was Mike not dead; he could still balance on a perch, walk around, and peck for food with a non-existent beak. He even made attempts at crowing. Olsen was so impressed with the rooster's resilience that he began caring for the disabled bird. He would feed Mike by squeezing liquidized food into the exposed neck using an eyedropper. A week later, Mike was still going strong.

An entertainment agent persuaded Olsen to take Mike on the road as a sideshow attraction. So Olsen had the bird insured for $10,000 and toured him around the country as Miracle Mike, charging 25 cents for a peek at the amazing headless chicken over the course of 18 months. The story soon spread nationwide, and photos of the bird standing next to his decapitated head were published in *LIFE* magazine.

Olsen took Mike to the University of Utah to figure out what was keeping the rooster alive. They deduced that while the axe blade had severed the front of the head and the beak, it had missed the jugular vein and most of the brain. A blood clot prevented Mike

from bleeding to death, and the remaining brain material was enough to support movement and vital mechanisms such as breathing.

Sadly, Mike choked to death in an Arizona hotel room in 1947. Nevertheless, he made such an impression in his short life that he was immortalized in a metal sculpture that still stands today in the center of Fruita, and the town's present-day residents remember him annually at the Mike the Headless Chicken festival.

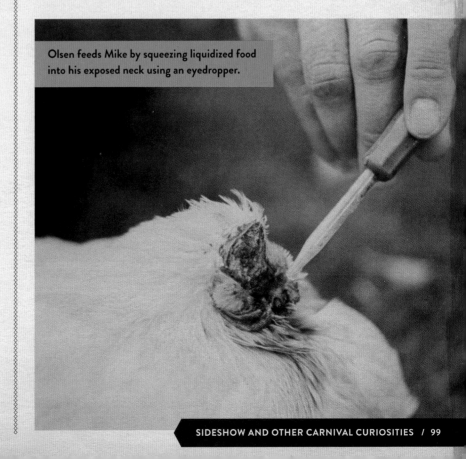

Olsen feeds Mike by squeezing liquidized food into his exposed neck using an eyedropper.

ELI BOWEN

BILLED AS: THE LEGLESS ACROBAT; THE HANDSOMEST MAN IN SHOWBIZ; THE WONDROUS MAN WITH FEET AND NO LEGS

Eli Bowen was born to parents Robert and Sarah on October 14, 1844, the only one of their ten children with a physical abnormality. His condition, a rare birth defect called phocomelia, left him with underdeveloped feet attached to his hips.

The Ohio native gained incredible upper body strength thanks to his inventive means of getting around. Bowen would walk on his hands using two wooden blocks, which kept his torso from dragging on the ground. Even when he reached his top weight of 140 lb (63.5 kg), he was able to pick himself up and walk in this way. Unhindered, Bowen helped around the family farm as a child, while also learning acrobatic tumbling stunts like cartwheels, somersaults, and backflips.

It is unclear exactly when he entered the sideshow world. Many reports state that he joined a small traveling circus at the age of 13, but records show he was attending school until at least 1860 and that he only started listing his profession as "showman" in 1870, five years after his father's death. He did eventually perform in most major shows, including the circuses run by Barnum & Bailey.

In addition to acrobatics, his act included a graceful pole routine, where he would climb to the top of a 13-ft (3.9-m) pole and perform stunts like spinning around from one arm while holding himself parallel to the ground. One of his most famous acts was a collaboration with The Armless Wonder, Charles Tripp. The two would ride a tandem bike together, with Tripp pedaling and Bowen steering.

The more he toured, the more admired he became, eventually earning the moniker "The Handsomest Man in Showbiz," and at 26 years old he married Mattie Haight (also known as Martha Haines), ten years his younger. The couple had four sons, none of whom were born with disabilities.

Despite earning a decent amount of money (at one time more than $100 a week, nearly $1,500 when adjusted for inflation), owning two farms, and having very financially successful sons, Bowen continued his act right up until the very end, suggesting he performed out of love for the craft and not necessity. He was still performing with The Dreamland Circus at Coney Island when he passed away at the age of 79 on May 4, 1924, from pleurisy.

CHANG AND
ENG BUNKER

BILLED AS: SIAMESE TWINS

Inspiring the term "Siamese Twins"—the rare condition being named after their birthplace, Siam (modern-day Thailand)—Chang and Eng are the world's most famous conjoined twins.

CHANG AND ENG BUNKER

Born in 1811 in a fishing village 60 mi (96.5 km) from Bangkok, twins Chang and Eng Bunker were connected by a small piece of cartilage at their sternum. But believe it or not, the rest of their systems operated completely independently from one another. So, even though their livers were fused, one could be intoxicated while the other was stone-cold sober—a good thing since Chang's weakness was alcohol. They both had their vices. Eng was known to go on gambling benders, playing poker all night long.

From a young age, their mother encouraged them to exercise, stretching their connecting tissue so that it gradually measured up to 5 in (12.7 cm), allowing the boys to have a little more wiggle room. Although very individual—Chang sported a bad temper (and was always a little shorter), whereas Eng was easygoing—the twins had inseparable experiences.

They were discovered by a Scottish merchant, Robert Hunter, who spotted the boys swimming. He realized their potential as a sideshow attraction in the West and paid their parents to take the 17-year-old brothers away as human oddities. They were poked by doctors and pointed at by spectators in their new home, with one doctor testing their connecting tissue with needles to determine sensitivity. Overcoming all medical odds and societal scoffs, Chang and Eng made the best of their unique condition.

Starting in 1829, they toured for about eight years, eventually ending their contract with Hunter and managing themselves for a time before settling down and enjoying life as southern gentlemen—plantation and all.

They had saved enough money, retired, bought and in North Carolina (even taking on slaves), and somehow, over the course of several years, managed to get to know two sisters—daughters of a respected local landowner. It was an unusual courtship: Chang and the allegedly "more attractive" sister, Adelaide, fell in love, while Eng and her sister, Sarah, were lukewarm. But in 1843, Chang and Eng married Adelaide and Sarah Yates, respectively.

The wedding stirred up scandal. People considered it "bestial"—a foursome at the very least. To that end, they all slept in an enlarged and strengthened marital bed built for four—Chang and Eng in the middle flanked their wives on either side. They lived in separate households on separate farms, taking turns spending a few days at each house. Chang and Eng never publicly discussed this private matter, but to put it in perspective, the couples both gave birth to their first children only six days apart. Chang and Eng fathered 21 children between them.

With the end of the Civil War came financial ruin for the Bunkers. They went back to the sideshow but had little success this time. Often taking two of their children on the road with them, the Bunkers were forced to come face-to-face with those who viewed their completely natural desire to pursue a normal family life as a devilish abomination.

While Eng was healthy, Chang's health deteriorated. Chang suffered a stroke in 1870, and in January 1874, during a bout of bronchitis, he passed away in his sleep. Awaking to find his dead brother attached to him, Eng panicked. A doctor was called to remove the dead brother, but Eng announced he was going too and died just two and a half hours afterward.

AVELINO PEREZ MATOS

BILLED AS: THE HUMAN EYE POPPER

Avelino Perez Matos was one of the earliest "eye poppers" featured in Ripley's Believe It or Not! He could bulge his eyes more than a centimeter out of their sockets at will, to the extent that it looked like his eyeballs would pop out at any moment. In 1928, Robert Ripley learned about the man from Baracoa, Cuba, with an astonishing ocular talent, and he featured Matos in the Believe It or Not! cartoon a year later. When selecting remarkable individuals for the first Odditorium in 1933, Ripley brought Matos from Cuba to perform as the "The Human Eye Popper," and his photographs—and a lifelike waxwork figure—have adorned Ripley's museums ever since.

The ability to roll back the eyelids in such a manner is known in medical circles as *exophthalmos*, and can be a symptom of various diseases. Fortunately, Avelino was perfectly healthy and didn't even need glasses!

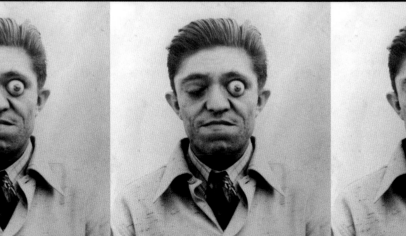

MARTIN EMMERLING

STAGE NAME: MARTIN LAURELLO

BILLED AS: THE HUMAN OWL

Martin Laurello, born Martin Emmerling in Germany in the 1880s, discovered an unnatural ability to rotate his head as a young man, and claimed to have spent three years perfecting the trick.

As the Human Owl (he was also known as Bobby the Boy with the Revolving Head), Emmerling was regularly featured on the European sideshow circuit. He could swivel his head a full 180 degrees, so that he could look directly over his own back while walking forward, all while dressed in his plain white shirt and slacks. The sideshow barker would loudly proclaim that he was only able to swivel his head so far by dislocating several bones in his neck! It's more likely that he was just extremely flexible.

Emmerling later took his act across the Atlantic in 1921, where he performed for the famous Ringling Bros. traveling circus, at Hubert's Museum in New York City, and at the famous Coney Island Dreamland fairground. In 1933, he was one of the stars to appear at the first-ever Ripley's Odditorium as part of the Chicago World's Fair. The Human Owl continued to be one of the biggest draws at Ripley's Odditoriums throughout the 1930s, and in 1940 he was one of the special guests pictured at a *LIFE* magazine party thrown by Robert Ripley at his island mansion in New York state.

In 1931, Emmerling abandoned his wife and moved to Baltimore. She retaliated by having the police fetch him, telling them to search for a man with a rotating head. Detectives combed the dime museums and carnivals and, funny enough, did find Emmerling— right in the middle of his act. He died of a sudden heart attack in 1955.

JULIA PASTRANA

BILLED AS: THE UGLIEST WOMAN IN THE WORLD; THE BEAR WOMAN; THE APE WOMAN; THE NONDESCRIPT

Julia Pastrana was a famous 19th-century performer, billed as "The Ugliest Woman in the World." Born in 1834 in Sinaloa, Mexico, Julia was covered from head to toe in thick black hair, a rare case of the genetic condition hypertrichosis. She also had protruding lips and gums—a result of gingival hyperplasia—and stood only 4 ft 5 in (1.35 m) tall. She spent most of her childhood in an orphanage, and then became a live-in entertainer and domestic servant for the state governor.

In 1854, at the age of 20, a customs agent persuaded Julia that she could make money from her curious appearance and brought her to New York City to be exhibited. There, Julia was described as resembling a bear or an orangutan, and nicknamed the "Semihuman" or "Ape Woman." She would sing in English and Spanish and dance for paying audiences and for scientists who were eager to examine her. One doctor declared her to be an entirely new species! However, Julia was far from the wild creature she was portrayed to be—she was a graceful dancer and spoke three languages. In New York, Julia met the showman Theodore Lent, who became both her new manager and her husband. Lent took Julia on a European tour, performing shows from London to Moscow, promoting her as a mysterious "Nondescript."

JULIA PASTRANA

In 1860, Julia became pregnant and, while in Moscow, gave birth to a boy, Theodore, who was also covered in hair. Tragically, he did not survive, and Julia passed away soon afterward. This should have put an end to Julia's remarkable journey, but after Lent had sold her body to a Russian university to be mummified, along with young Theodore, he decided that the show must go on and took the preserved corpses back on the road. Mother and son spent the next few decades being exhibited in a glass cabinet at sideshows around Europe, finding their way to Norway in the 1920s, where they were displayed until the 1970s, before being looted by fairground vandals. Sadly, Theodore was too damaged to be saved, but Julia, despite her arm being ripped off by the vandals, was rescued by the Oslo University Hospital, where she was placed in storage until 2013, when her story took one more incredible twist.

At the request of the Mexican government and following a long-standing campaign from visual artist Laura Anderson Culebro, Julia's body was repatriated to her hometown in Sinaloa, where she was finally laid to rest in a Catholic funeral, more than 150 years after her death.

JORGE ROBLES

STAGE NAME: CHICLE

Born on January 22, 1990, in Puerto Rico, Jorge Iván Latorre Robles has some very unusual talents—he can stretch his skin, pop out his eyes, and dislocate his joints.

He didn't discover his talents until he was 18, when he was breakdancing and found that his flexibility allowed him to perform tricks unlike the other dancers. Robles was soon diagnosed with Ehlers-Danlos syndrome, a condition that affects his body's production of collagen (which provides strength and structure to the skin), causing the skin to loosen.

Earning the nickname and stage name "Chicle" (meaning "chewing gum" in Spanish), Robles honed his skills at the Puerto Rican Theater Improvisation League (Liga Puertorriqueña de Improvisación Teatral) and the Time Machine Squad dance group before following in the footsteps of other stretchy, "elastic" men in sideshows.

Robles mostly uses his talents to entertain people, performing at theaters, working as a street performer, and volunteering at the hospital to entertain sick children, who often think he is a superhero with stretchy skin powers.

Ehlers-Danlos syndrome is a rare inherited condition that affects the connective tissue in the body. Connective tissue helps support the skin and bones and is composed of cells, fibrous materials, and a protein called *collagen*, which acts as a bodily "glue." More than 80 percent of the skin is made up of collagen. People with Ehlers-Danlos syndrome suffer from a defect in collagen production, and this weakening of the connective tissue can result in highly elastic skin.

Lewis was often paired with Johanna Dickens, known as the Bear Girl. Dickens had a normal torso and short, thick legs. They were sometimes billed as the Most Unusual Sisters in the World, or even described as cousins. Neither claim was true.

ALZORIA LEWIS

BILLED AS: THE TURTLE GIRL

Human oddities and sideshow performers were the celebrities of Coney Island. Alzoria Lewis, billed as the Turtle Girl, worked at Coney Island from the 1930s to the 1950s.

In 1912, Alzoria was born with all of her limbs stunted; she had six fingers on each hand and six toes on one foot and one toe on the other. Her short legs gave her a standing height of just 2 ft (0.61 m) tall. Her act consisted of her crawling around on all fours and sharing the sad, sordid story of her past, struggling to grow up disabled in the South. She would peddle her autographed pitch cards—the equivalent of sensational baseball cards—to the sympathetic crowds.

In reality, Alzoria was born and raised in Brooklyn and made enough money working at Coney Island in the summer months to live comfortably all year with her boyfriend. She eventually married twice, and it's believed at least one husband married her for her money.

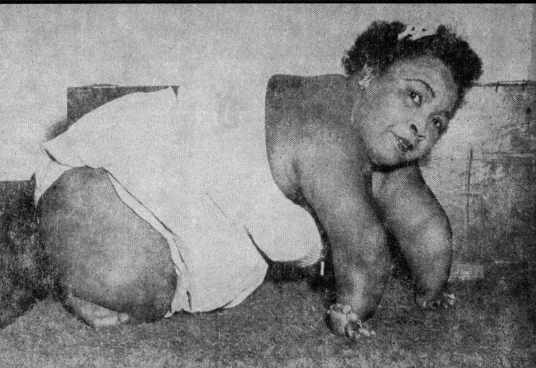

OTA BENGA

Born in 1883, Ota Benga, of the Mbuti pygmy tribe from the Congo, was ripped from his home in 1904 and brought to the United States to be displayed as a human zoo exhibit.

Amid European intervention in Africa, Ota Benga returned from an elephant hunt as a teenager to find his family and village slaughtered. He was soon kidnapped by slave traders. American missionary and amateur anthropologist Samuel Phillips Verner negotiated his release, essentially buying him for a pound of salt and a bolt of cloth (or some brass wire, as other sources state).

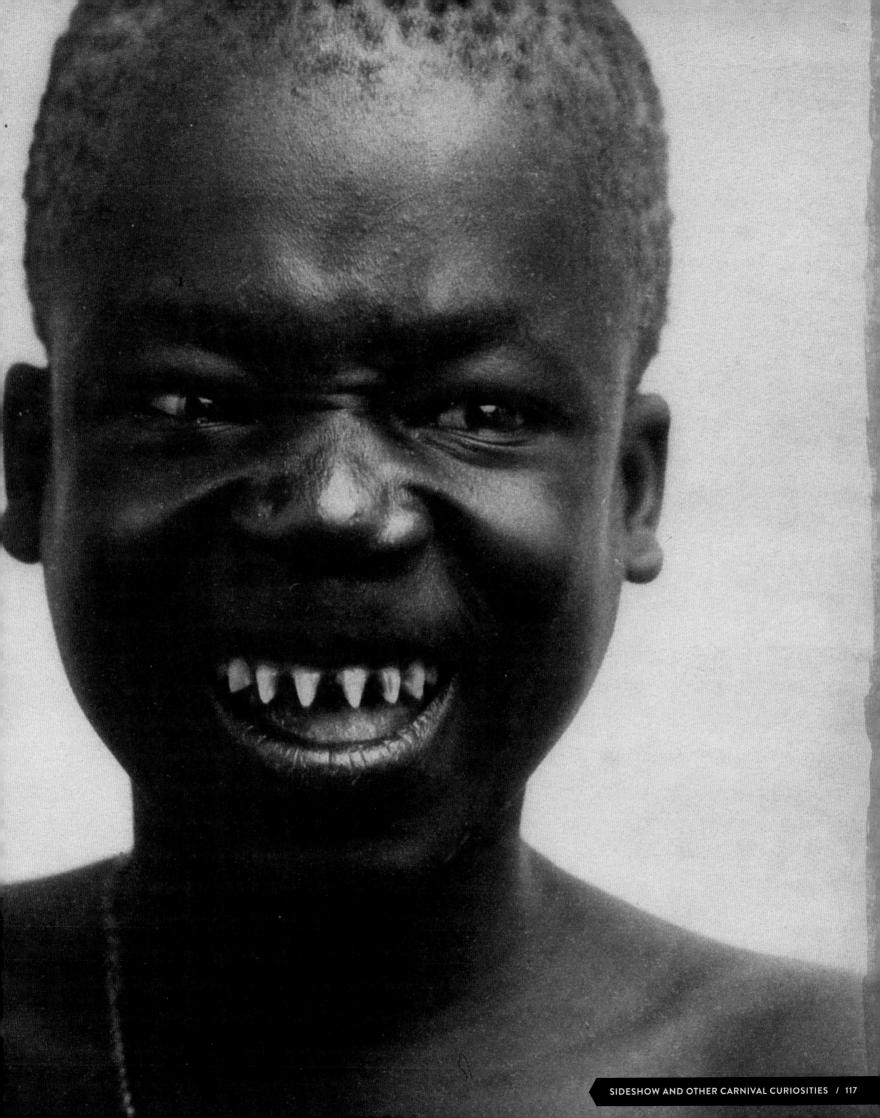

Benga shared his space with an orangutan whom he became quite attached to.

OTA BENGA

Since Verner was a recruiter for the Louisiana Purchase Exposition, Ota Benga was initially on display at the St. Louis World's Fair with completely different tribes as part of an ethnological exhibit. Standing only 4 ft 11 in (1.22 m) tall and weighing 103 lb (47 kg), with his teeth ritually filed down to sharp points, Benga was the biggest draw, attracting gawkers from around the world.

Two years later, after returning to Africa and feeling out of place, Benga was back in the states, this time working at the New York Zoological Gardens, now known as the Bronx Zoo, helping with the animals. Zoo officials, however, noticed large crowds coming to see Benga and forced him to live on display as an animal exhibit.

Housed in the primate house, Benga entertained visitors—500 people at a time—by shooting a bow and arrow, weaving, and interacting with the other animals in his enclosure. In 1906, as many as 40,000 people flocked to Benga each day.

After a group of black clergymen demanded he be freed, Ota Benga went to live in Lynchburg, Virginia. He capped his teeth, changed his name, and began working at a local tobacco factory, trying to save enough money to travel back to his homeland. But when World War I broke out, travel became near impossible. Ota Benga committed suicide on March 20, 1916. He was 33 years old.

Ota Benga stands second from the left at the 1904 World's Fair, also known as the Louisiana Purchase Exposition.

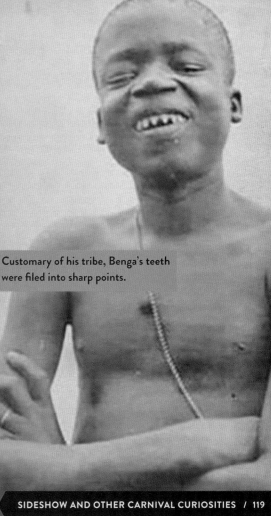

Customary of his tribe, Benga's teeth were filed into sharp points.

STEPHAN BIBROWSKI

STAGE NAME: LIONEL

BILLED AS: THE LION-FACED MAN

Born circa 1891 near Warsaw, Poland, Stephan Bibrowski's lion-like appearance was the result of a thick covering of fur across his face and body.

STEPHAN BIBROWSKI

At the age of four, Bibrowski's parents allowed Sedlmayer, a German impresario, to take Stephan under his charge and exhibit him in Europe. By 1895, the hairy boy's career officially began. Of course, he needed a stage name and backstory, and Sedlmayer obliged willingly. But Sedlmayer also ensured that the boy received a thorough education. This would become an important component of his later stage persona.

Bibrowski transformed into "Lionel, the Lion-Faced Boy," a child whose mother had watched her husband get maimed and eaten by a lion while pregnant. The resulting abomination was too much for her to handle. While none of this backstory was founded in reality, it made for an effective gimmick.

In reality, Bibrowski suffered from a condition known as hypertrichosis, resulting in abnormal hair growth across his body. As an infant, the hair measured about 1 in (2.5 cm) long. But by the time he started working the freak-show circuit, it had grown to 8 in (20.3 cm) on his face and 4 in (10.1 cm) across the rest of his body. The only exceptions were the palms of his hands and soles of his feet.

He stood a diminutive 5 ft 3 in (1.6 m) tall and had a slight build. Like others with hypertrichosis, he only developed a couple of teeth. Intellectually, however, he proved brilliant. He was well-educated and spoke five different languages. By some accounts, he hoped to become a dentist one day.

Bibrowski toured extensively across Europe and later added America to his schedule. In 1901, at the age of 10, he joined the Barnum & Bailey Circus as a replacement for Jo-Jo the Dog-Faced Boy. He toured with them extensively across the United States. Besides awing crowds with his wild appearance and highly educated bearing, he also performed acrobatics.

In 1907, he moved to Germany and enjoyed fame at the Passage-Panoptium Wax Museum for a handful of years before relocating to New York in 1913. For the next 15 years, he performed at Coney Island's Dreamland Circus sideshow to adoring crowds.

He passed away in Germany in 1928 of a heart attack. Bibrowski has since been inducted into Coney Island USA's Sideshow Hall of Fame.

LIONEL
LION FACED BOY

FRIEDA PUSHNIK

BILLED AS: THE ARMLESS, LEGLESS GIRL WONDER

Half-girl Frieda Pushnik was born on February 10, 1923, in Conemaugh, Pennsylvania, without arms or legs—a product of a botched appendectomy on her pregnant mother—yet could accomplish common tasks without assistance.

Although she had a happy childhood, the family was destitute and accepted an offer from Robert Ripley to perform at his Odditorium in 1933. Aged just ten years old, she wowed audiences at the Chicago World's Fair with her cheerful repartee. Her act consisted of sitting on a pillow and speaking to the audience; explaining what she can do; and, of course, demonstrating writing, threading needle, sewing, and using scissors.

The pitch card she sold at her shows said her hobbies were "painting, music, reading, movies, crocheting, sewing, and most everything as a normal person." She also made a point of saying, "I need no assistance at mealtime ([and] can handle silverware, glasses, cups, etc.), apply my own makeup, brush my own teeth, do all my own letter writing, can type, and have won several penmanship awards."

For six years Frieda performed as "Little Frieda Pushnik, the Armless, Legless Girl Wonder" in Ripley's Believe It or Not! Odditoriums and then went on to have a successful sideshow career with Ringling Bros. and Barnum & Bailey Circus before retiring from the stage in the 1950s.

In December 2000, Pushnik died in her home at the age of 77 after battling bladder cancer.

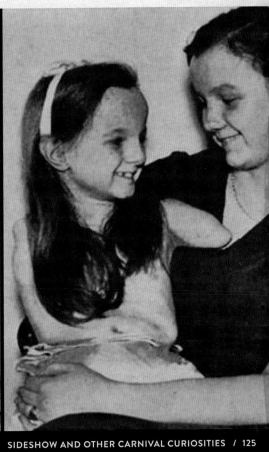

GEORGE AND WILLIAM MUSE

STAGE NAME: EKO AND IKO

BILLED AS: MEN FROM MARS; AMBASSADORS FROM MARS

Blue-eyed Eko and Iko were prized circus acts—musicians dressed in strapping outfits that showcased their wild white dreadlocked hair. At various points in their career, they were Ecuadorian cannibals, "Sheep-Headed Men," "Monkey Men," or "Sheep-Headed Cannibals." It was claimed that John Ringling discovered the twins floating off the coast of Madagascar. At another point, newspapers touted that the pair were found in 1923 in the Mojave Desert, where their spaceship crash-landed, and thus their most famous moniker stuck: "Ambassadors from Mars" or "Men from Mars."

GEORGE AND WILLIAM MUSE

Their real names were George and Willie Muse, two brothers (not twins) with albinism from Truevine, Virginia, who were born in the 1890s and grew up on their sharecropper family's tobacco farm. As the story goes, in 1899, as they were working in the fields, the boys were abducted by circus promoter James Herman "Candy" Shelton, who enticed them with a piece of candy and forced them into the circus.

There is some evidence that points to their mother, Harriet, contracting the boys with a traveling carnival operator, casting doubt on whether Candy Shelton kidnapped the boys later than 1899. One thing is certain—the boys were missing by 1914, and Shelton was acting as their touring manager as they made their way through showman Al G. Barnes's circus and eventually Ringling Bros. and Barnum & Bailey Circus. The brothers picked up playing the mandolin and guitar, among other instruments, and were able to play a tune after just hearing it once.

However, they were kept uneducated; were not paid wages; and to keep them complacent, were told their mother was dead. She was not.

In autumn 1927, the brothers traveled to Roanoke, Virginia, as part of the Greatest Show on Earth. Their mother, despite being illiterate, learned that the circus was in town, telling relatives that it came to her in a dream. And just as her boys were playing "It's a Long Way to Tipperary," they noticed a familiar woman who had elbowed her way to the front of the crowd. "There's our dear mother," George reportedly said. "Look, Willie, she is not dead."

The family was reunited after almost 13 years. The tender reunion was punctuated by Sheldon (their abductor and manager), circus executives, and city cops converging and intimidating Harriet Muse into not reclaiming her sons. But she persisted, and the family went home together that day. Three days later—in a time and place where KKK rallies were common and Jim Crow laws legalized racial segregation—Harriet hired a white lawyer to file a lawsuit against the legendary circus for her sons' back wages.

After winning a settlement, the boys ended up returning to the circus in 1928, but this time on their own terms. They performed at Madison Square Garden, which drew thousands of spectators, and later toured Europe, Asia, and Australia, making enough money over the years to send some back home. Harriet continually looked out for her sons, ensuring the circus made good on its promises, and she saved enough money to purchase a farm in Franklin County, a place where her sons could retire.

In 1942, at the age of 68, she passed away, and in 1961, George and Willie Muse finally retired. They sold the property their mother purchased for them and bought a house in Roanoke, Virginia, in 1961—an incredible achievement for any African American of the era. The brothers never married but were cared for by the women in their family. George died in 1971, while Willie lived to be 108, passing away in 2001.

The Muse brothers were thought to have been mentally incompetent, but that was not the case, as they were never taught to read or write and their eyesight was deteriorating as a result of their albinism.

ARE THEY AMBASSADORS FROM MARS?

ARE THEY AMBASSADORS FROM MARS?

CHRIS AND ELAINE STEELE

STAGE NAME: CAPTAIN AND MAYBELLE

Chris and Elaine Steele, of Atlanta, Georgia, have been performing classic sideshow stunts as vaudeville couple Captain and Maybelle for more than 17 years, setting world records along the way and capturing the world's attention on *America's Got Talent*, season 6.

Their show includes a variety of feats, including eye-socket weight lifting, glass eating, fire breathing, human suspension, and of course, sword swallowing. A fixture during yearly World Sword Swallower's Day festivities, Chris became the new record holder for "weighted sword swallowing" when he downed a 17-in (43-cm) blade with 84 lb (38 kg) of weights attached.

It took about 4 ½ years before Chris was able to swallow a sword successfully, and learning the stunt wasn't without its injuries. When asked why they started sword swallowing and performing other classic sideshow acts, Chris said, "When I was young, I would go to the carnival, and I was fascinated with the entertainers, from fire breathers to sword swallowers. But I was more fascinated once I knew it was real, that it wasn't an illusion. In my mind, if they could do it, I could do it."

Elaine, aka Maybelle, swallows and eats a whole balloon.

"IF I CAN GET A LAUGH OUT OF SOMEBODY, THAT'S WHAT I WANT, AND IF HE CAN MAKE THEM CRINGE, THEN THAT'S WHAT HE WANTS."

—ELAINE

Swallowing 13 swords.

Chris, aka Captain, uses his eye sockets to lift a bucket holding a 10-lb (4.5-kg) brick.

Electricity flows through his body and out of the sword to light Elaine's torch.

JEAN-FRANÇOIS GRAVELET

STAGE NAME: CHARLES BLONDIN

BILLED AS: THE GREAT BLONDIN

Charles Blondin was born Jean-François Gravelet in 1824 in France. He grew to be only 5 ft 5 in (1.7 m) tall and 140 lb (63.5 kg), but he is considered the world's greatest tightrope walker (funambulist) of the 19th century.

JEAN-FRANÇOIS GRAVELET

Gravelet's father was a tightrope walker himself, as was his father before him (who was known as a "rope dancer"), and as a young boy Gravelet attended a gymnastics school. Beginning his career as an acrobat when he was just four years old, it took Gravelet a mere six months to premiere as "The Little Wonder." His skill at gymnastics and natural affinity for grace quickly propelled him into the spotlight. He became known as the Great Blondin for his signature blond hair.

It's thought that by the end of his career Gravelet had covered 10,000 mi (16,000 km) on perilous tightropes around the world. He never used a safety line and never relied on a net—he thought to do so would be to tempt fate. His only concessions to safety were guy ropes, supporting lines fixed to the ground, which prevent the main tightrope from swinging around too much in the wind.

When Gravelet announced his Niagara stunt, nobody expected him to actually complete the walk. But on June 30, 1859, thousands of people thronged the banks of the Niagara Gorge to watch agog as the greatest stuntman in the world walked 1,100 ft (335 m) across the Niagara River on a tightrope only a few inches thick. He carried only a long balancing pole for assistance; there was no safety line or net to catch him if he fell roughly 175 ft (53 m) into the swirling waters below.

The crowd gasped as he stooped in the middle to haul up a bottle of wine from a boat far below, take a glug, and then continue to the other side. But the Great Blondin wasn't finished; after a quick rest, he completed the return journey back across the river, this time carrying a camera, and he stopped to take a picture of his audience en route.

The Frenchman made headlines on both sides of the Atlantic. Gravelet returned to Niagara on several more occasions. On each walk the master strove to eclipse his previous walks, upping the ante by completing the walk backward, hanging from the tightrope with his hands, dressing up as a gorilla, wearing a sack over his head, being locked in manacles like a prisoner, performing backward somersaults, and balancing on his head for minutes at a time.

In 1859, Blondin carried his manager, Harry Colcord, across Niagara Falls on his back, telling Colcord, "If I sway, sway with me. Do not attempt to do any balancing yourself. If you do we will both go to our death." In 1860, he pushed a man across the river in a wheelbarrow. He once famously carried a table and chairs onto the rope, then sat down to enjoy a meal and bottle of wine. He went further still when he carried an iron stove across the rope on his back, stopping in the middle to make an omelet. He then lowered the dish to spectators on a boat below.

ANNIE JONES

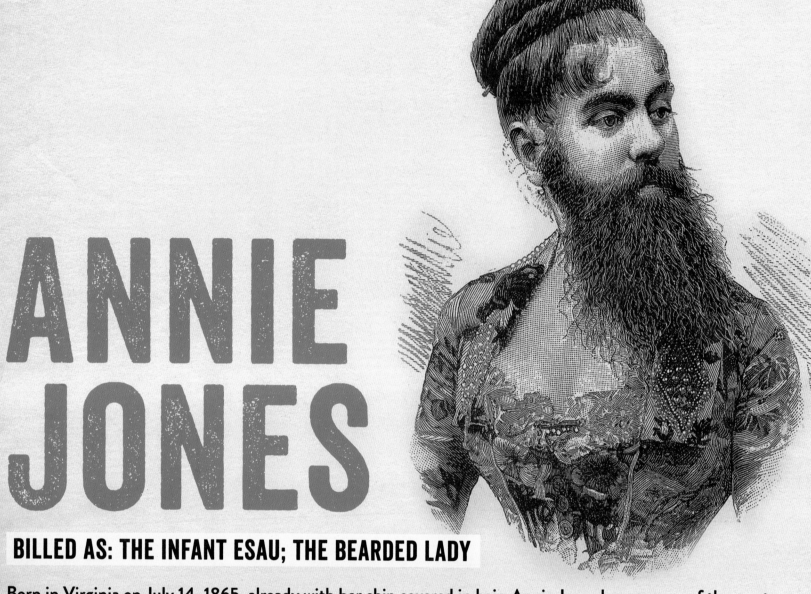

BILLED AS: THE INFANT ESAU; THE BEARDED LADY

Born in Virginia on July 14, 1865, already with her chin covered in hair, Annie Jones became one of the most famous bearded ladies of the sideshow era.

Although her parents were stunned at their daughter's hairy appearance, they quickly capitalized on the opportunity. She was barely a year old when she started touring with P. T. Barnum—her parents received an exorbitant $150 a week for her appearance. She was billed as "The Infant Esau," a reference to the Old Testament biblical figure Esau, Jacob's brother, who was famously hairy. Sporting a full mustache and sideburns by the age of five, not to mention her mandolin-playing musical talent, she was easily one of Barnum's prized acts.

In 1881, she married sideshow barker Richard Elliot—she was only 16. After 14 years of marriage, the couple called it quits. Not long after the divorce, Jones married again to a William Donovan (some say her childhood sweetheart), and the pair traveled to Europe, touring as a duo. Donovan unexpectedly died four years later, leaving Jones a widow and with no choice but to rejoin the the Greatest Show on Earth. During this time, at the peak of her popularity, she utilized her sideshow platform to campaign against and discourage the use of the word "freaks."

On October 22, 1902, Jones passed away, at the age of 37, of tuberculosis. It is unclear if Jones's condition was caused by hirsutism (unwanted, male-pattern hair growth in women, usually on the face, chest, and back) or some other genetic condition.

French poster advertising Annie Jones as "The Bearded Lady."

STANISLAUS BERENT

STAGE NAME: SEALO, THE SEAL BOY

Born with no arms, Stanislaus Berent's hands grew directly from his shoulders like a seal's flippers, but he didn't let this stop him from leading a full, independent life.

Berent suffered from a condition known as phocomelia, which can result from chemical exposure or, in Berent's case, a rare congenital condition. Discovered on the streets of Pittsburgh selling newspapers, he took the stage name "Sealo, the Seal Boy" when he joined the circus. Phocomelia roughly translates as "seal arms."

During his performances, Sealo performed routine activities, such as shaving, without the use of full-length arms. When needed, he used a stick-and-hook contraption, rendering him capable of completing nearly any task. But it was Berent's warm, gracious personality that endeared him to fans and helped him sustain a career spanning more than three decades.

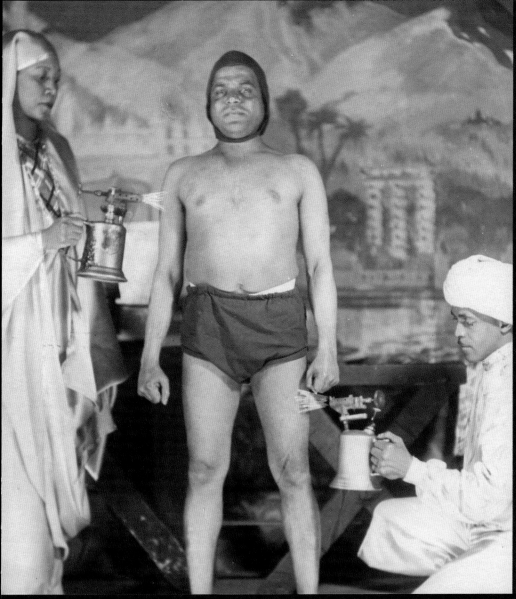

KUTTY SINGLEE

BILLED AS: THE FIREPROOF MAN

Kutty Singlee claimed that he could not be harmed by fire and regularly took blowtorches to his bare skin and even eyes to prove his point.

Fire plays an important role in traditional Hinduism as both the creator and destroyer of life. It's an integral part of ceremonies throughout India, ranging from cremation to weddings, sacrifices to offerings. The element is embodied in the Vedic fire god, Agni.

Said to be a devotee of Agni, Singlee came from Solon, India. He created a carnival act that represented far more than a simple parlor trick. Exposing his nearly naked body to fire before stunned crowds, he remained unharmed. According to some, he argued that his show was an act of religious faith, but skeptics saw it as little more than a clever illusion.

In 1934, he performed at the Chicago Odditorium for Robert Ripley, quickly garnering the title of "The Fireproof Man."

JUMBO THE ELEPHANT

In the 1880s, the most popular and iconic attraction at P. T. Barnum's newly minted circus was Jumbo the elephant, who sadly met a tragic end.

Jumbo the African elephant was born on his home continent in 1860, but when his mother was killed by hunters, he was taken and sold to the highest bidder. Jumbo ended up a main attraction at the famed London Zoo, spending nearly 17 years at the institution and, because of his gentle disposition, giving hundreds of children rides on his back around the grounds.

BARNUM, BAILEY & HUTCHINSON CHALLENGE THE WORLD IN $100,000,00, that JUMBO is the Largest & Heaviest Elephant ever seen by mortal man either wild or in captivity.

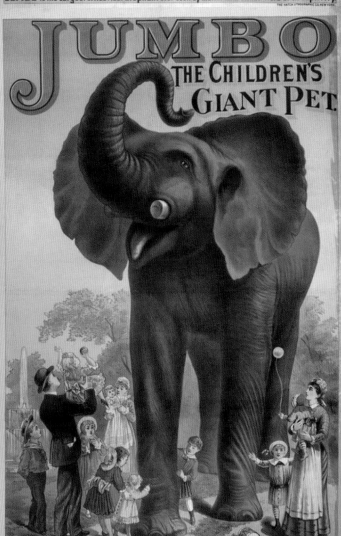

JUMBO THE CHILDREN'S GIANT PET.

BARNUM, BAILEY & HUTCHINSON CHALLENGE THE WORLD IN $100,000,00, that JUMBO is the Largest & Heaviest Elephant ever seen by mortal man either wild or in captivity.

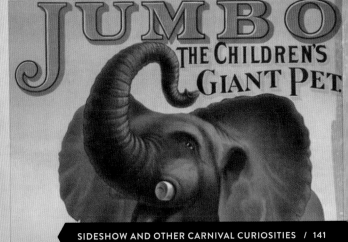

JUMBO THE CHILDREN'S GIANT PET.

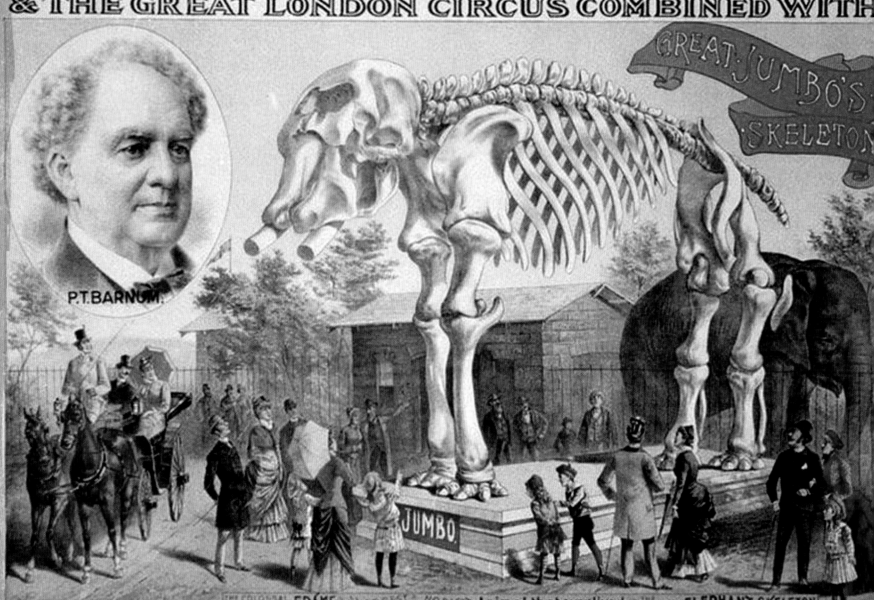

P.T. BARNUM & CO'S GREATEST SHOW ON EARTH
& THE GREAT LONDON CIRCUS COMBINED WITH

GREAT JUMBO'S SKELETON

P.T.BARNUM.

JUMBO.

THE COLOSSAL PRODIGIOUS FRAME LARGEST NOBLEST Animal that ever lived. ONLY ELEPHANT SKELETON ever publicly exhibited. A STRANGE & AMAZING SHOW WITHOUT A PARELLEL MOUNTED BY PROF. HENRY A WARD THE DISTINGUISHED NATURALIST & SCIENTIST OF ROCHESTER N.Y.

SANGER'S ROYAL BRITISH MENAGERIE & GRAND INTERNATIONAL SHOW

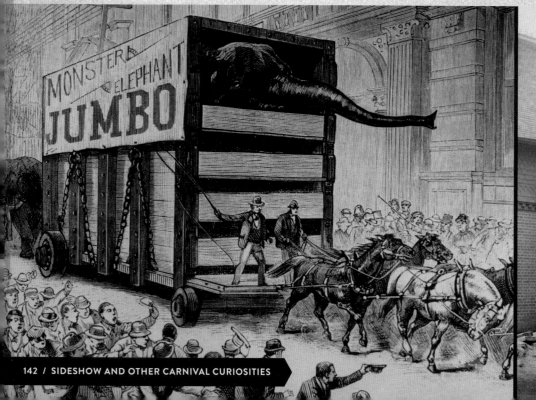

MONSTER ELEPHANT JUMBO

JUMBO THE ELEPHANT

Despite being portrayed as a nice elephant giving joy to the zoo's youngest visitors, Jumbo was beaten by his captors and fed alcohol-soaked biscuits to keep him calm. He developed an alcohol problem, with his keepers even touting that he loved whiskey and champagne.

Soon zoo officials became concerned about the animal possibly injuring guests when cute little Jumbo had a growth spurt. In the early 1880s, he was sold to P. T. Barnum for $10,000. This caused an uproar in England, with a sudden outpouring of interest and sympathy for poor Jumbo, even from Queen Victoria. To make matters worse, Jumbo reportedly had to be chained up and dragged into the small iron box that would transport him to the United States.

Weighing 7 tons and standing nearly 13 ft (3.9 m) tall, the colossal pachyderm became a larger-than-life institution, a symbol of the circus, no doubt because of Barnum's impeccable marketing campaign. He garnered endorsement deals with his celebrity status, and even his name—which was a combination of two Swahili words, "Jumbe" for chief and "Jambo!" as a greeting—became synonymous with anything large in size.

Jumbo traveled with the circus for just three years. During the circus show, he was often paired with a small elephant named Tom Thumb in a classic sideshow-style giant-and-midget routine. The animal abuse, however, never subsided—he was hit with sledgehammers, spears, and bull hooks to keep him in line.

In 1885, Jumbo was struck by an unscheduled freight train while crossing some train tracks in Canada and died. His longtime trainer Matthew Scott had tried to rush the elephants off the tracks to no avail. Barnum had Jumbo's hide stuffed and his skeleton wired together, so he still profited from his star attraction for a few more years. Barnum also spun the train accident into a fantastical story, claiming that Jumbo had pushed Tom Thumb off the tracks thereby sacrificing himself.

Today, Jumbo is the official mascot of Tufts University, and his stuffed hide stood in Barnum Hall until 1975. Jumbo is also believed to be the inspiration behind Walt Disney's 1941 animated feature *Dumbo*.

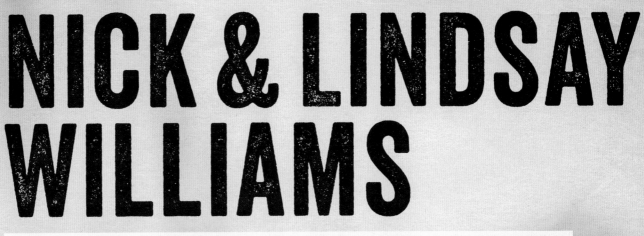

NICK & LINDSAY WILLIAMS

STAGE NAME: GUGLIELMO "THE OPERA SINGING DAREDEVIL,"

AND MADAME DAGGERS "THE DANGEROUS DAME OF DAGGERS"

BILLED AS: SIDESHOW OPERA

Classically trained musicians Nick and Lindsay Williams of New Orleans, Louisiana, combine their musical talents with dramatic acts such as glass walking, eating razor blades, and throwing knives—with their feet.

Nick (aka Guglielmo) also swallows razor blades on a chain, although he is extremely careful to not damage his vocal cords, as he feels his voice comes first before any sword swallowing or glass eating.

Lindsay (aka Madame Daggers) was inspired by armless knife thrower Paul "Judge" Desmuke, who was featured in Ripley Odditoriums in the 1940s.

NICK & LINDSAY WILLIAMS

Nick, who also goes by his stage name Guglielmo "The Opera Singing Daredevil," first combined singing and sideshow in 2014. Nick's intense vocal training included his teacher stacking heavy books on his diaphragm to build breath support, which has led to Nick being able to sing opera while Lindsay uses a sledgehammer to smash a cinderblock on his chest as he's lying on a bed of nails.

Early on in the development of their act, Lindsay would accompany Nick by playing the violin, but she soon wanted a circus talent of her own. In 2016, she found her calling in knife throwing and became so proficient that she could throw with her feet.

Her stage name reflects her ability—Madame Daggers "The Dangerous Dame of Daggers."

When asked what inspired them to combine sideshow with opera, they said, "We both find that the dramatics of classical music go very well theatrically with the dramatics and emotions that sideshow and circus acts create. We wanted to make classical music and opera more accessible to all ages and walks of life." The couple has taken their musical sideshow act across the country, having found a way to combine their love of music, each other, and history into one-of-a-kind performance art.

Erlich stands with fellow performer Clarence Chesterfield Howerton, aka Major Mite.

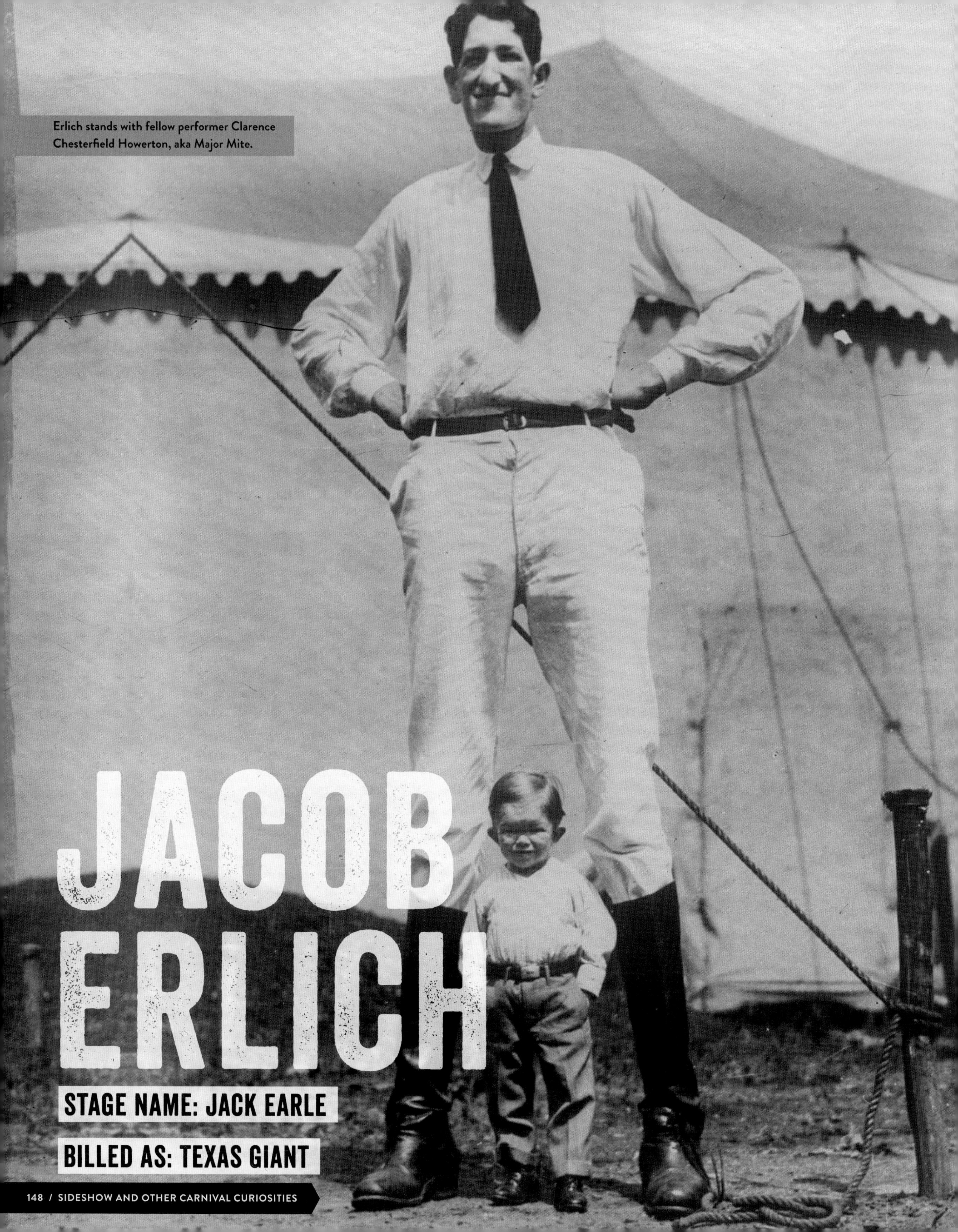

JACOB ERLICH

STAGE NAME: JACK EARLE

BILLED AS: TEXAS GIANT

Although Jacob Rheuben Erlich weighed just 4 lb (1.8 kg) when he was born in Denver in 1906, by 17, he towered above the masses, measuring 8 ft 6 in (2.6 m) in height.

The son of German Jewish immigrants, Erlich was discovered by Hollywood during a trip to Los Angeles with his dad. Taking the screen name of Jack Earle, he appeared in 48 films along with celebrities such as famed child star Baby Peggy. From *Hansel and Gretel* (1923) to *Jack and the Beanstalk* (1924), Erlich's movie career proved successful.

But during filming for his 49th movie, he fell 14 ft (4.2 m) from scaffolding and was knocked unconscious by falling timber. He awoke in the hospital with blurred vision and a cracked nose. Over the next three days, his vision continued to diminish until he went blind.

While examining the giant, his doctor found a tumor growing on his pituitary gland. The tumor had gotten pushed forward during the fall and was placing pressure on his optic nerve; it was now affecting his vision. After four months of X-ray therapy, Erlich's eyesight returned. Some people have also theorized that Erlich stopped growing as a result of the doctor's intervention.

Erlich joined Ringling Bros. and Barnum & Bailey Circus in El Paso, Texas, after his friends challenged him to check out Jim Tarver. Tarver was touted as the tallest man in the world. To his delight, Erlich measured a good 13 in (33 cm) taller, and he was hired on the spot. He would tour with the Ringling Bros. into the early 1940s, before starting his own sideshow.

DAISY AND VIOLET HILTON

BILLED AS: THE UNITED TWINS; THE HILTON SISTERS; THE BRIGHTON TWINS; THE BRIGHTON CONJOINED TWINS

"THE SENSATION OF VAUDEVILLE"

San Antonio's

SIAMESE TWINS

DAISY and VIOLET HILTON

BORN JOINED TOGETHER

DAISY AND VIOLET HILTON

Despite being conjoined twins, Daisy and Violet Hilton (1908–1969) overcame numerous obstacles to lead independent lives and earn their keep in show business.

The twins were born in Brighton, England, to Kate Skinner, an unmarried barmaid. According to the *British Medical Journal*, they were delivered by physician James Augustus Rooth. At the time, Rooth noted that they were the first set of British conjoined twins to survive past a few weeks. Joined at the hips and buttocks, the twins shared no major organs. However, Rooth would rule out operating to separate them. Because they shared blood circulation, he felt the procedure was too risky and could result in the death of one, if not both, of the twins.

Assisting with the birth was Mary Hilton, Kate Skinner's employer. Realizing the twins had commercial potential, Mary talked Kate into selling them to her. This marked the beginning of an abusive home life for the twins. Yet, it also proved instrumental in preparing them to be performers.

The twins lived with Mary, her husband, and their daughter. According to Daisy and Violet, they lived in constant fear of abuse. Forced to call Mary "Auntie Lou" and her husband "Sir," the girls were controlled, manipulated, and exploited by the Hiltons.

Nonetheless, the Hiltons also were crucial to their development as entertainers. They provided the girls with dancing and singing lessons. These skills proved priceless in the world of vaudeville, sideshows, and burlesque.

In 1911, the girls were first exhibited in the UK as "The United Twins." They were three years old. Mary later took them on tours of Germany and Australia, before visiting the United States for the first time around 1916.

Despite becoming one of the most popular acts of their day—even performing with Bob Hope—the twins remained impoverished. All of their earnings were kept by their handlers. In other words, Daisy and Violet lived in virtual slavery.

Their bleak situation was exacerbated by the death of Mary in Birmingham, Alabama. Instead of finding the freedom they longed for, the girls were bequeathed to Mary's daughter and her husband, Edith and Meyer Meyers. The sisters ping-ponged back and forth between fame, isolation, and abuse at the Meyers's San Antonio, Texas, mansion. During this time, they received jazz lessons: Daisy became a violinist and Violet a skilled saxophonist.

In 1931, the twins made a life-changing decision. They sued the Meyers, gaining their freedom and $100,000 in damages. Reinventing themselves as "The Hilton Sisters' Revue," they joined the vaudeville circuit. Daisy dyed her hair blond, and they began wearing different outfits for the first time in their lives.

Their romantic lives became fodder for the press from 1932 onward. Violet fell in love with musician Maurice Lambert. They applied for marriage licenses in 21 states but to no avail. That same year, the girls starred in *Freaks* (1932) with other famous sideshow performers such as the Snow siblings. In 1941, they followed up with the exploitative film *Chained for Life*, loosely based on their lives.

As early as 1932, their fame started to wane. By 1961, their manager quit. The twins ended up working at a grocery store for the rest of their lives. In January 1969, they died within a few days of each other, victims of the Hong Kong flu, and are buried in the Forest Lawn West Cemetery in Charlotte, North Carolina.

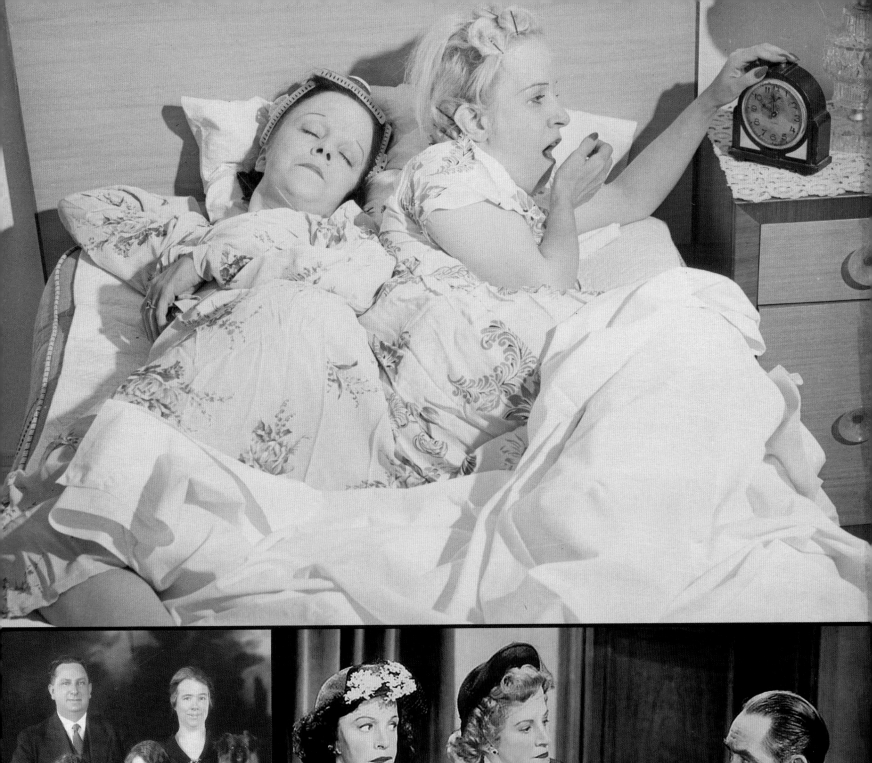

The twins posing with the Meyers.

ISAAC SPRAGUE

BILLED AS: LIVING HUMAN SKELETON; THE ORIGINAL THIN MAN

Born in 1841 in Massachusetts, Isaac W. Sprague was by all accounts a normal boy, until he started mysteriously losing weight at the age of 12. The sudden weight loss, despite his healthy appetite, left doctors stumped.

Unable to hold a stable job due to his weakened condition, Sprague joined the circus sideshow in 1865 and toured on and off with P. T. Barnum for years billed as "The Living Skeleton" and "The Original Thin Man." In February 1868, at the age of 26, he married 16-year-old Tamar P. Moore, and the couple had three perfectly healthy children.

At 44, Sprague was 5 ft 6 in (1.7 m) tall and weighed just 43 lbs (19.5 kg). Unfortunately, Sprague passed away at the age of 45, on January 5, 1887, of asphyxiation, probably as a complication of his condition. The living skeleton act went on to become a sideshow staple, purely because of Sprague's great popularity, and the act soon expanded, pairing fat ladies with skeletal men.

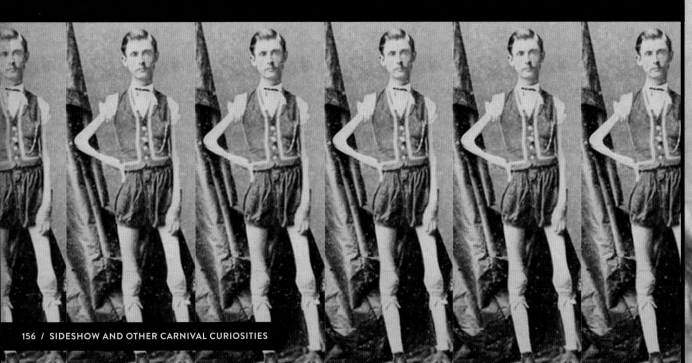

THE LUCASIE FAMILY

STAGE NAME: THE WONDERFUL ELIPHOBUS FAMILY; THE WONDERFUL ALBINO FAMILY

BILLED AS: WHITE MOORS

According to P. T. Barnum, Rudolph Lucasie and his family were "White Moors" from Madagascar with their pale skin, silken ivory hair, and pink eyes being markers of a newly discovered race.

THE LUCASIE FAMILY

In their own right, the Danish Lucasie family was an impressive sight to behold. Barnum first discovered them at the Amsterdam Fair in 1857. Sensing plenty of potential, he quickly added them to his slate of sideshow acts.

Never much for truth telling, Barnum concocted wild tales about the family's origins. He refashioned them as an endangered, indigenous people native to Madagascar. In one text, he even discussed their pink eyes, claiming the Lucasies didn't need to close them at night while sleeping. In an age defined by exoticism and Social Darwinism, the Lucasies' true identity as Europeans simply wouldn't do.

By 1860, they appeared in New York City at Barnum's American Museum. Barnum also circulated a preposterous, pseudo-scientific pamphlet about the family. In the pamphlet, Rudolph was referred to as a "handsome specimen of the human variety." The work tells a fanciful, fictional tale of the family's Madagascan origins. Using the term "White Moors," Barnum attempted to distinguish them from other albino performers of the time.

A famous portrait by Currier and Ives of "The Wonderful Eliphobus [literally 'fear of the sun'] Family" was commissioned, and the family's fame skyrocketed.

The Lucasies' career spanned a combined 40 years. During this time, Rudolph, his wife Antoinette, and their children entertained countless crowds. Besides Barnum, they performed with W. W. Coles and the Lemon Brothers. After the death of Antoinette, Rudolph continued touring on the vaudeville circuit. He worked as an albino violinist until his death in Kansas City, Kansas, in 1909.

GRACE MCDANIELS

BILLED AS: THE MULE-FACED WOMAN

Grace McDaniels was born in 1888 in Iowa, with the birthmark that would define her career. As an adult, her face was swollen with protuberances and extremely large lips, creating a striking countenance that earned her an unfortunate moniker: "The Ugliest Woman in the World."

After winning an "ugliest woman" competition, McDaniels joined a traveling sideshow and began a successful entertainment career. She would climb the sideshow platform wearing a heavy veil and only show her face after a build-up from the master of ceremonies, who told the waiting audience, "You will see the Mule-Faced Woman, Grace McDaniels, the only living lady in all the world who was born with the face of a mule." When Grace finally removed the veil—which she didn't wear offstage—it's said that men and women would faint at the sight of her deformity. Nevertheless, she preferred to be called the "Mule-Faced Woman," rather than the "Ugliest Woman in the World," and that's how she became known.

McDaniels's unusual appearance is thought to have been caused by either the rare congenital disorder Sturge-Weber syndrome, which causes deforming birthmarks, or elephantiasis of the lip. She once told a newspaper, "My remarkable facial condition is a birth mark, due to a confusion in the capillary, arterial, and nervous systems previous to my birth. I lead a normal life—prefer housekeeping, although the show life is an enjoyable one and healthful." She toured for decades as the Mule-Faced Woman, but perhaps her biggest gig was performing at the first Ripley's Believe It or Not! Odditorium, at the 1933 Chicago World's Fair.

Despite her unusual appearance, Grace did not lack for romantic attention and had a son named Elmer, who later became her manager. She would spend winters in Gibsonton, Florida, renowned as a town where traveling sideshow and circus performers spent the off-season. Grace shared the town with many well-known performers, including Grady "Lobster Boy" Stiles, Al "The Giant" Tomaini, and Percilla the Monkey Girl.

McDaniels with her son Elmer, who was perfectly healthy and later became her manager.

Here McDaniels poses with her sideshow family.

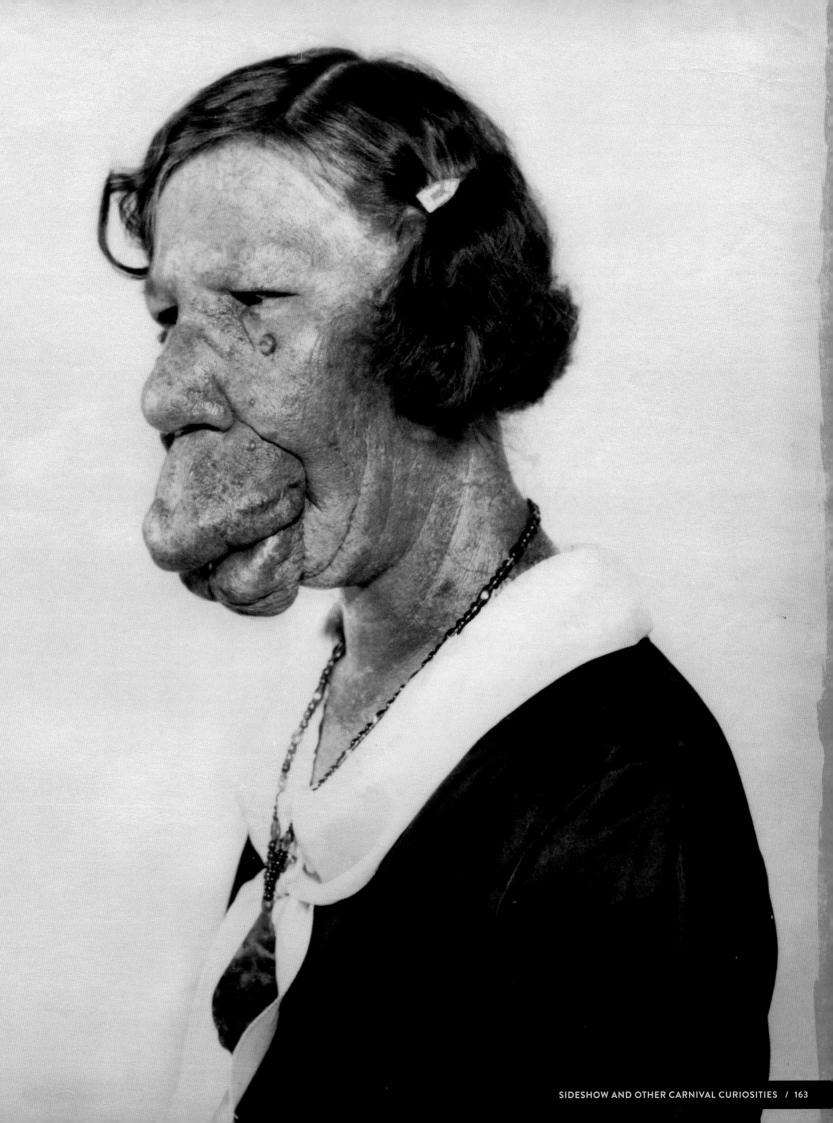

MARÍA JOSÉ CRISTERNA

BILLED AS: VAMPIRE WOMAN

María José Cristerna, a mother of four and former lawyer from Mexico, has had almost 50 body modifications in order to transform herself into the Vampire Woman.

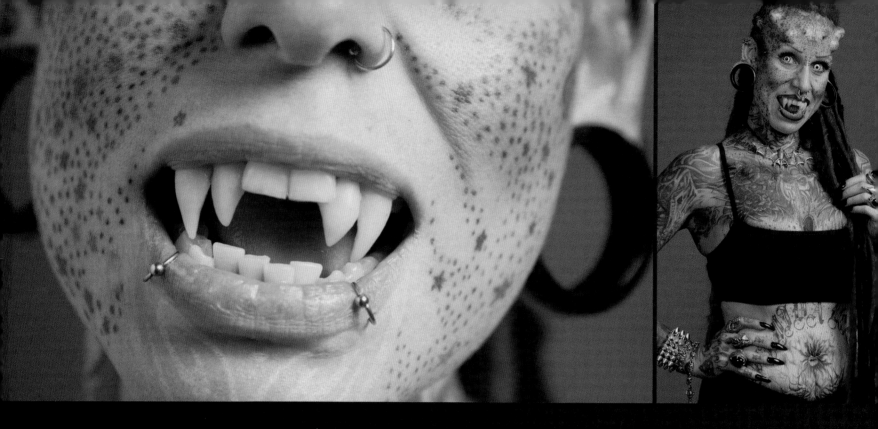

MARÍA JOSÉ CRISTERNA

Cristerna started her transformation with a piercing, then gauged ears when she was 12 years old. From there on out, it was a gradual modification to include many piercings, tattoos covering more than 90 percent of her body, large earlobe tunnels, permanent fangs, and transdermal (under the skin) implants on her head, chest, and arms that include horns made from titanium.

The tattoo artist considers her tattoos a part of her and would never consider removing any. "It would be like trying to erase something that's already been lived, and, well, it's impossible; everything is a story."

Cristerna told Ripley's that she reinvented herself as "Vampire Woman" as a sign of strength after troubles in her life. When Ripley's asked what she hopes to achieve by her unusual appearance, Cristerna simply said, "To be no one but me, really. Never, never did I want to please nor displease anyone, simply be free to express and feel what I want... We classify beauty like we want and we look for the stereotype we want; beauty is subjective."

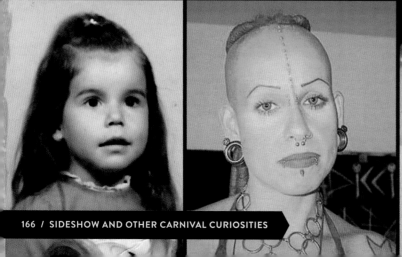

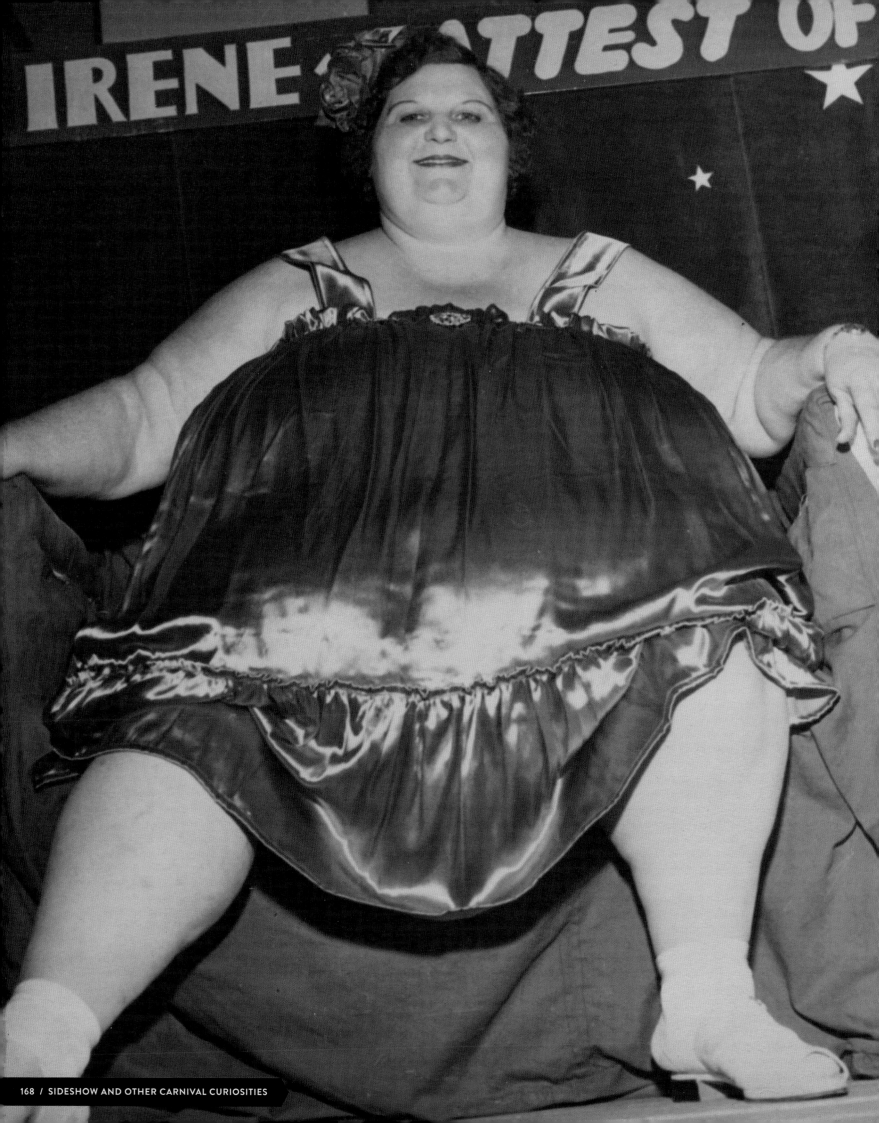

AMANDA SIEBERT

BILLED AS: BABY IRENE; JOLLY IRENE

"Baby Irene" gifted the circus sideshow with her massive girth and infectious sense of humor, becoming one of the most beloved fat ladies to ever grace the stages of the Ringling Bros. or Coney Island.

Born in 1880 in Jersey City, New Jersey, Amanda Siebert was anything but jolly or jiggly in her youth. In 1901, at the age of 21 years old, she weighed a slim 120 lb (54.4 kg), and the last thing on her mind was becoming a circus performer.

But after she became pregnant and had a baby, her weight skyrocketed. Blaming hormonal and glandular changes brought on by pregnancy, she packed on the pounds, climbing to a hefty 689 lb (312.5 kg). After people started laughing when they saw her, she decided to join the circus so that she could at least make some money in the process.

Although it was common for fat performers to use the term "jolly" as a part of their stage name, "Baby Irene" had a jovial stage presence that audience members and the media loved. She was also a self-professed fan of chocolate and bananas but would eat anything in sight.

After growing too large to ride on passenger trains across the country with the Ringling Bros., she confined herself to summer performances in New York with them. The rest of the year she spent performing at Coney Island. She died in 1940 of a heart attack related to morbid obesity.

MILLIE AND CHRISTINE MCCOY

BILLED AS: THE TWO-HEADED NIGHTINGALE; CAROLINA TWINS

Millie and Christine McCoy were born joined at the hip to slaves on a farm in North Carolina in 1851, the eighth and ninth of 14 siblings.

MILLIE AND CHRISTINE MCCOY

While still toddlers, they were sold to a traveling show and traded between various showmen before Joseph Smith became their manager. In another trade gone wrong, the sisters were stolen and taken to England, where they were abducted at least once more, before Smith and the girls' mother, Monemia, tracked them down four years later. When they were eventually returned to the United States, Smith and his wife helped Millie and Christine learn to sing, dance, and play the piano and guitar, promoting them as the "Two-Headed Nightingale"—one with a contralto voice, the other a soprano.

The pair also mastered up to five languages and wrote their own poetry, talents that helped make the girls international stars. At the height of their popularity, "Millie Christine"—the girls would often refer to themselves as a single person—was performing for thousands of people each day, and 150,000 spectators saw the pair over the course of eight weeks when they visited Philadelphia. They soon earned enough money to buy a farm in North Carolina with their father Joseph—then a free

man—and to support schools for black children. They performed at P. T. Barnum's American Museum in New York and appeared before Queen Victoria of England on a number of occasions.

They retired from show business by the early 1900s, and survived until 1912 when they contracted tuberculosis and died within 24 hours of each other. They are buried at Welches Creek cemetery, North Carolina, where their descendants held a ceremony in 2012 to honor the centenary of their death.

Millie and Christine were joined at the pelvis, making them "Pygopagus" twins, a relatively rare form of the condition with two separate bodies (most conjoined twins share organs or are joined at the head). It is plausible that Millie and Christine could have been separated with modern medical techniques, but medical knowledge at the time was limited and the twins were very happy regardless to live together as one, having once written, "We would not wish to be severed, even if science could effect a separation."

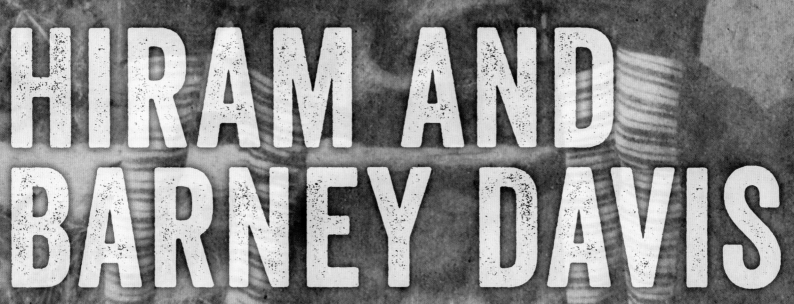

HIRAM AND BARNEY DAVIS

STAGE NAME: WAINO AND PLUTANO

BILLED AS: THE WILD MEN OF BORNEO

From their backstory to their names and even their spoken tongue, everything about the "Wild Men of Borneo" proved to be a gimmick.

Each man stood about 3.5 ft (1 m) tall and exhibited extraordinary levels of strength. Known as Waino and Plutano, they kept their hair long and unkempt, acted feral, and spoke in a strange gibberish that anthropologists and linguists found impossible to crack. And with good reason.

Almost nothing about the dynamic duo, apart from their height, turned out to be true. In reality, the Wild Men of Borneo were two brothers named Hiram and Barney Davis, and their real background proved anything but exotic. Hiram was born in 1825 in England, and his brother Barney was born two years later in New York.

Discovered by a traveling showman named Doctor Warner in the early 1850s, he wove many tall tales about their discovery and subsequent capture by sailors in Borneo. But the devil is in the details, and many of Warner's didn't line up.

The savviest newspaper reporters had their doubts, decrying the two performers as little more than dwarves from the United States. Yet, despite the accurate press, audiences continued to flock to their shows. By 1874, the Wild Men of Borneo act was valued at $50,000.

In 1882, they toured with P. T. Barnum. Over the next quarter century, they earned $200,000. On stage, they regaled crowds with stories of their legendary past and performed various feats of strength, which included lifting a purported 300 lb (136 kg) apiece.

FRANCESCO LENTINI

STAGE NAME: THE GREAT LENTINI

BILLED AS: THE THREE-LEGGED MAN; THE THREE-LEGGED WONDER

Known as "The Three-Legged Wonder," Francesco "Frank" Lentini (1889–1966) had three legs, four feet, and two sets of genitalia due to a parasitic twin joined at the base of his spine.

Frank Lentini enjoyed many stage names, including "The Great Lentini," and he toured with countless circuses throughout his career. Born on a farm in Rosolini, Sicily, he was the fifth of Natale and Giavanna Falco's 12 children. Initially rejected by his parents, he was shipped to his Aunt Giacoma and Uncle Corrido Falco's household for safekeeping. At the age of four months, he was taken to a specialist in Naples, but no medical interventions were possible.

By the age of five, Frank could stretch his third leg, although walking with it proved impossible. Despite his deformities, he played with other children and remained in good health. In 1898, he was exhibited with a traveling puppet show in Middletown, and his family accompanied him. After this experience, Natale and Giavanna decided to immigrate to the United States. This move had a huge impact on Frank's budding career.

Soon, he performed with the Ringling Bros. Circus, touring the country to great success. Part of his act involved kicking footballs into the crowds who flocked to see him. In 1906, he made his big debut with the Barnum Circus at Madison Square Garden in New York City.

He married Theresa Murray in 1907, and they had four children together. They separated in 1935, and he went on to live the rest of his life with Helen Schupe. During a career that spanned more than 40 years, Frank performed with Buffalo Bill's Wild West Show and Barnum & Bailey, among others. He garnered much respect and admiration from his peers and, as a result, was referred to as "The King."

WANG

STAGE NAME: THE HUMAN UNICORN

In 1930, an expat Russian banker sent Robert Ripley a photo of a Chinese farmer from Manchukuo with a nearly 14-in (35.6-cm) horn-like spire growing from the back of his head.

Ripley was intrigued by the image, dubbing the unknown Chinese farmer "The Human Unicorn." According to the photo, the farmer in question was normal physiologically, apart from the cranial protrusion.

Beyond a basic idea of the farmer's location, Ripley only knew that the man went by Wang or Weng. To track down the horned gentleman and learn more about his abnormal feature, Ripley posted a huge cash reward for anyone who could assist in arranging an appearance of "The Human Unicorn" at the Ripley's Believe It or Not! Odditorium.

Unfortunately, Ripley's curiosity would never be satisfied. Following the announcement of the reward, the man in question disappeared from the public eye. His whereabouts were never located. But the mystery of his strange growth has most likely been solved.

Doctors believe Wang's horn was the result of calvarial tumors or osteomas. In rare cases, these growths can manifest as an aggressive variant known as cornu cutaneum. They can occur anywhere on the body. Today, modern medicine has led to the near eradication of horned humans because these individuals get diagnosed and treated early.

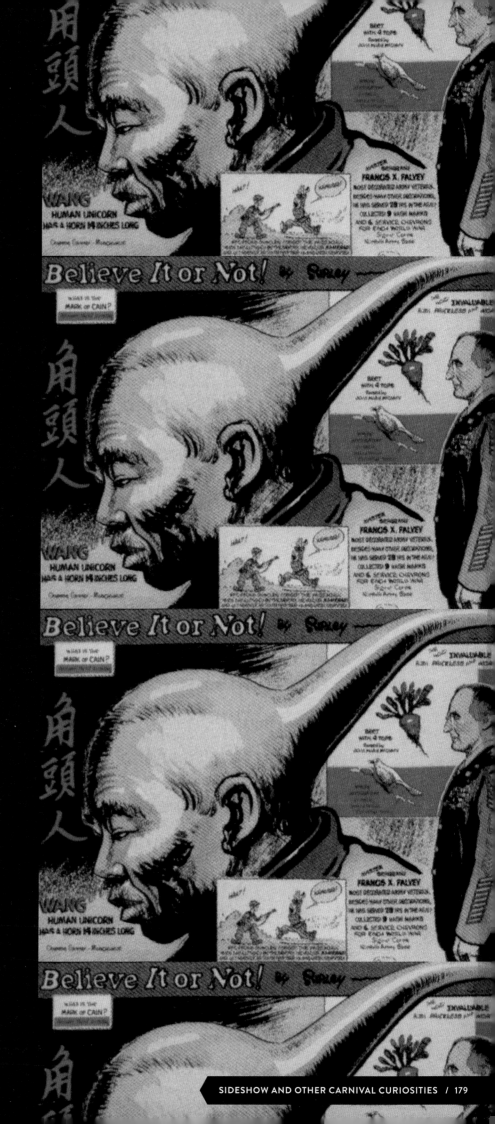

ASHBURY BENJAMIN

BILLED AS: LEOPARD BOY; THE PIEBALD BOY

Ashbury Benjamin was an African American performer exhibited as the "Leopard Boy" due to a rare skin condition (vitiligo) that made his skin look patchy.

In the 1870s and 1880s, the "Piebald Boy" (as Benjamin was also known) enjoyed fame on the freak-show circuit. A regular with P. T. Barnum, Benjamin performed alongside veteran circus performers. This included William Henry Johnson, known as "Zip the Pinhead." In the 1880s and 1890s, Ringling Bros. and Barnum & Bailey featured the "Ash and Zip" act, where the two performers staged a fake boxing match.

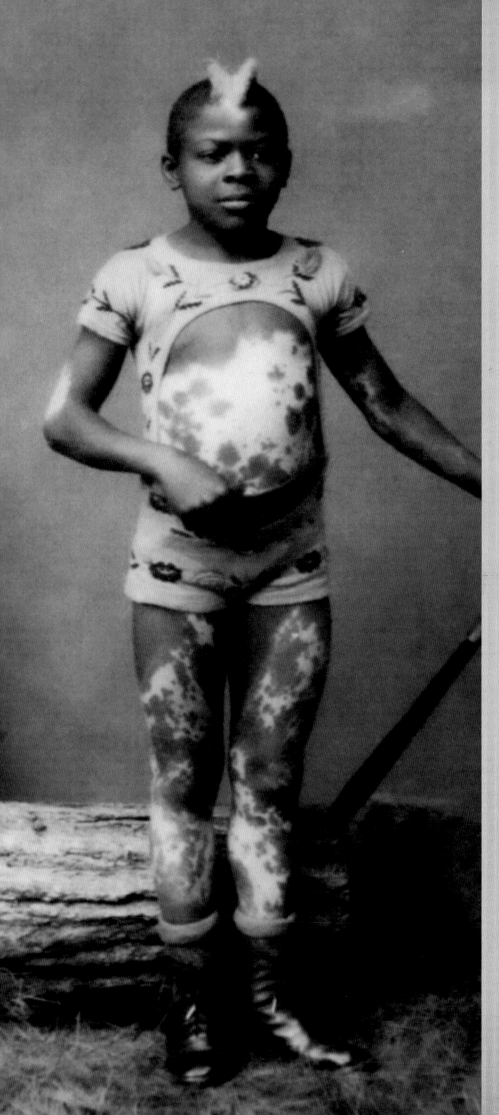

ROYAL AQUARIUM
G. A. FARINI'S
LEOPARD BOY!
Spotted Black, White and Yellow, from Head to Foot.

FEDOR JEFTICHEW

STAGE NAME: JO-JO THE DOG-FACED BOY

Fedor Jeftichew was born in Russia in 1868. He exhibited the genetic condition hypertrichosis passed on by his father, which caused thick hair up to 8 in (20 cm) long to grow all over his face.

As a child, Fedor was exhibited with his equally hairy father, Adrian, in European sideshows as a cross between a human and a bear. (Adrian had distanced himself from civilization and was an alcoholic forest hermit.) Some claim that Fedor and Adrian were examined by scientists who thought they might be a long-lost race of men. They returned to Russia in the 1870s and, after Adrian died, the orphaned Fedor made his way back into the spotlight, exhibiting in St. Petersburg (Russia), Berlin (Germany), and eventually London (England).

In England, he came to the attention of P. T. Barnum, who in 1884, invited Fedor, nicknamed Jo-Jo, then aged 16, to the United States. He was soon performing in the Barnum & Bailey Circus at New York's Madison Square Garden as "Jo-Jo the Dog-Faced Boy." Barnum described Fedor as "the human Skye terrier" and claimed that the boy had been captured by a hunter who found him living in the wild in a Russian forest cave, a tall tale designed to make him sound more frightening. Fedor was happy to play along with the story, snarling and growling like a wolf on stage, despite wearing a sharp, ornate Russian military uniform. In reality, he could speak perfectly well in English, Russian, French, and German.

Fedor continued to tour throughout the 1880s and '90s and was well paid, earning $500 a week, at least 20 times more than the average person. He continued performing until his death from pneumonia, in Greece, in 1904.

The P.T. Barnum Performers (from left to right): LALOO, Eight-limbed Man; YOUNG HERMAN, Expanding-Chest Man; J. K. COFFEY, Skeleton Man; JAMES MORRIS, Stretchy-Skin Man; JO-JO, The Dog-Faced Boy.

Fedor (left) and his father, Adrian (right).

MINNIE WOOLSEY

STAGE NAME: KOO KOO THE BIRD GIRL

Koo Koo the Bird Girl, blind and toothless, with her small head, thin face, and beaky nose, was a well-known character on the circus sideshow circuit in the early 20th century.

She was born Minnie Woolsey in Georgia in 1880, and it's said that she was discovered by a shrewd showman in a Georgia insane asylum. She became a fixture for many years in the Ringling Bros. Circus sideshow. Minnie's act, complete with fluffy feathers and oversized chicken feet, consisted of dancing strangely and acting foolish before the crowd.

In 1932, her unique appearance earned her a role in Tod Browning's film *Freaks*, featuring an ensemble cast of bizarre sideshow workers, and she was performing as the "Cuckoo Girl" at the World Circus Sideshow at Coney Island, New York, into the 1940s.

Unlike many of her outlandish colleagues, Minnie was quiet and reserved away from the stage and did not draw attention to herself until dressed in her feathers. It's likely that she suffered from a type of dwarfism called Virchow-Seckel syndrome, also known as "bird-headed" dwarfism.

It's unknown how long Minnie was with the circus or when she died. There is one account that says she was nearly run over by a car in 1960, which would mean she was still alive at 80 years old.

Despite having no lines in *Freaks*, Minnie is well remembered for dancing on the table—in full costume complete with a feathered cap and chicken feet—during the wedding feast of Cleopatra (the trapeze artist) and Hans (the dwarf).

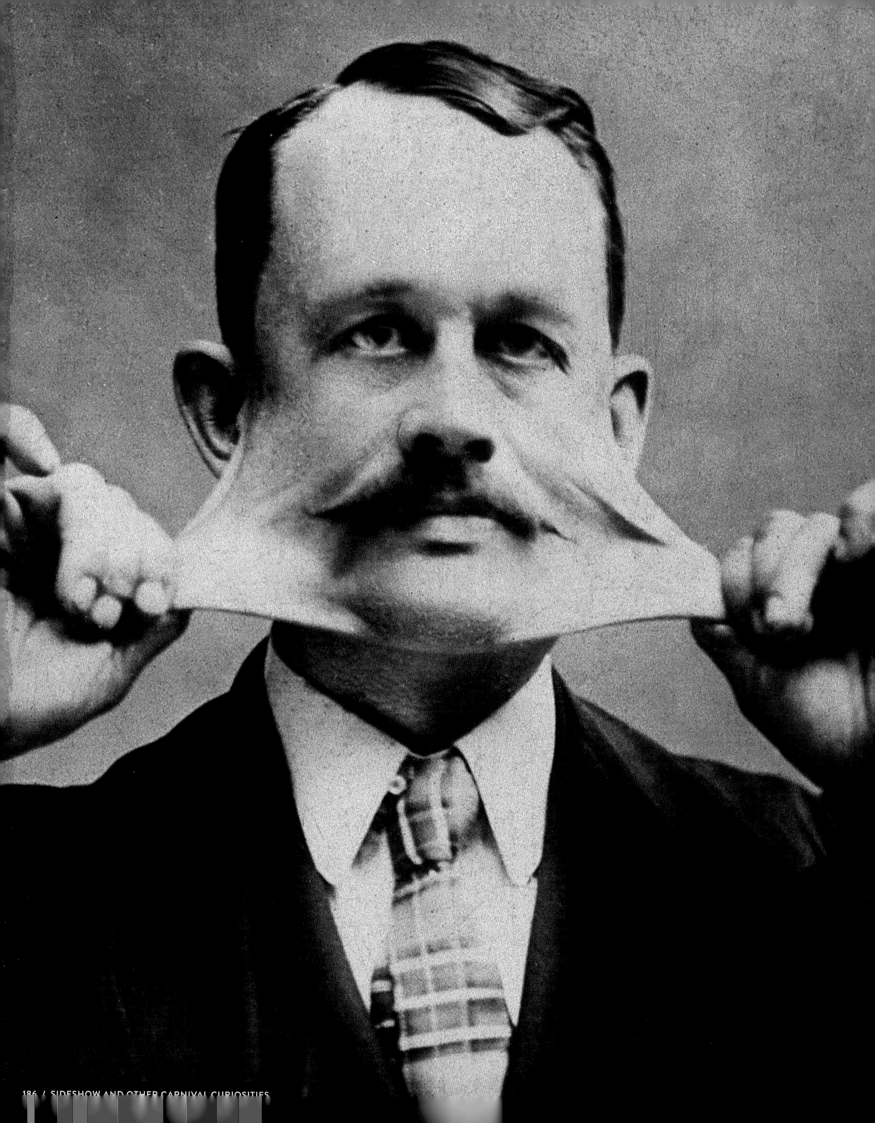

JAMES MORRIS

**BILLED AS: THE RUBBER MAN;
THE ELASTIC MAN**

Born in 1859 in Copenhagen, New York, James Morris could stretch the skin on any part of his body to incredible lengths, thanks to the disorder called Ehlers-Danlos syndrome.

He went from stretching his skin for the amusement of his friends and coworkers to performing at dime museums and eventually Barnum & Bailey shows for a reported $150 a week. He unsurprisingly was known as "The Rubber Man," due to his skin's hyper elasticity. It's said that he could pull the skin as much as 18 in (45.7 cm) away from his body without experiencing any pain. His most well-known trick was pulling the skin of his neck up over his nose.

Rumor has it that when his fame dwindled, he became an alcoholic gambler and earned extra money as a barber, even owning his own shop in New York City. Not much is known about the last years of Morris's life, although he did have at least one other contemporary—the "Elastic-Skin Man" by the name of Felix Wehrle, about whom next to nothing is known. Both Morris and Wehrle sported beards, the same inherited ability, and ran in the same sideshow circles, making historical photo identification of either man quite difficult.

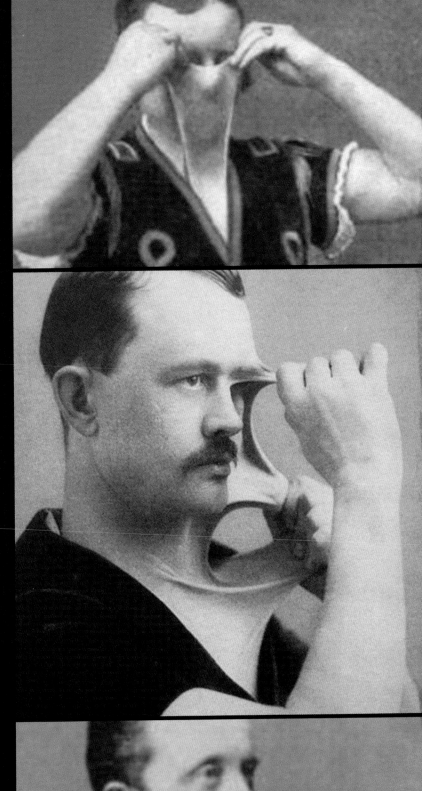

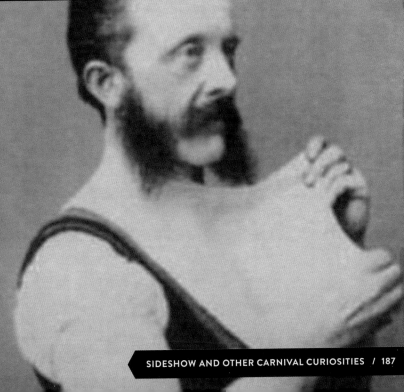

JOSEPH MERRICK

BILLED AS: THE ELEPHANT MAN

Joseph Carey Merrick was born August 5, 1862, in Leicester, England, and showed no signs of his eventual deformity. He was a kind and sympathetic individual, not to mention intelligent; he was literate and could read and write.

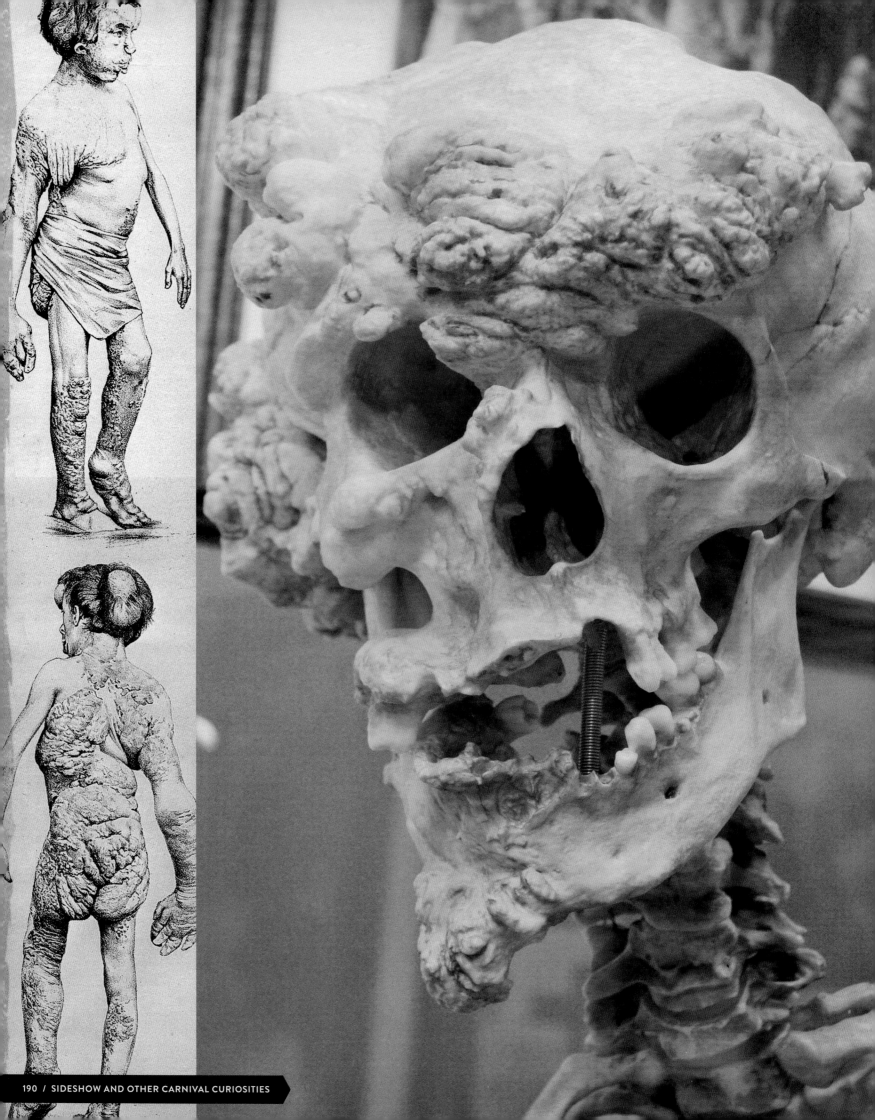

JOSEPH MERRICK

At the age of five, abnormal growths of skin and bone began to cause severe disfigurement in Merrick. His head grew to 3 ft (9.8 m) in circumference, while his right wrist measured 1 ft (0.3 m) in circumference; puckered skin hung from his head, face, and body; with a twisted hip, he was only able to walk with the help of a cane; and with all this, he could barely speak or show expression on his face.

Merrick escaped working in a brutal workhouse by the age of 22 and found work in the traveling freak show, where he became known as "The Elephant Man." His health worsened during his time on exhibition, and when he was robbed of all his money while on tour, he made his way back to Britain and into the care of Doctor Frederick Treves at the Royal London Hospital. He gained a measure of fame back in Britain, especially among London society, and received many visitors, including Alexandra, Princess of Wales.

He remained in the hospital until his death on April 11, 1890; he died in his sleep of asphyxia at just 27 years old. Although Merrick spent his later years in the care of doctors, no one was able to confirm what genetic defect he suffered from. For a long time, people thought he suffered from an extremely severe case of neurofibromatosis, but it's likely he had the rare disease known as Proteus syndrome.

Since his death, Merrick has attracted even more attention: Bernard Pomerance wrote a play about his tragic life, aptly named *The Elephant Man*, which appeared in 1979 and is still being performed today. Most famously, director David Lynch produced a film in 1980 starring Anthony Hopkins and John Hurt, who played Merrick. In the 1980s, Michael Jackson reportedly tried to buy his bones from the Royal London Hospital after being touched by Merrick's sad story and visiting his skeleton, then on display.

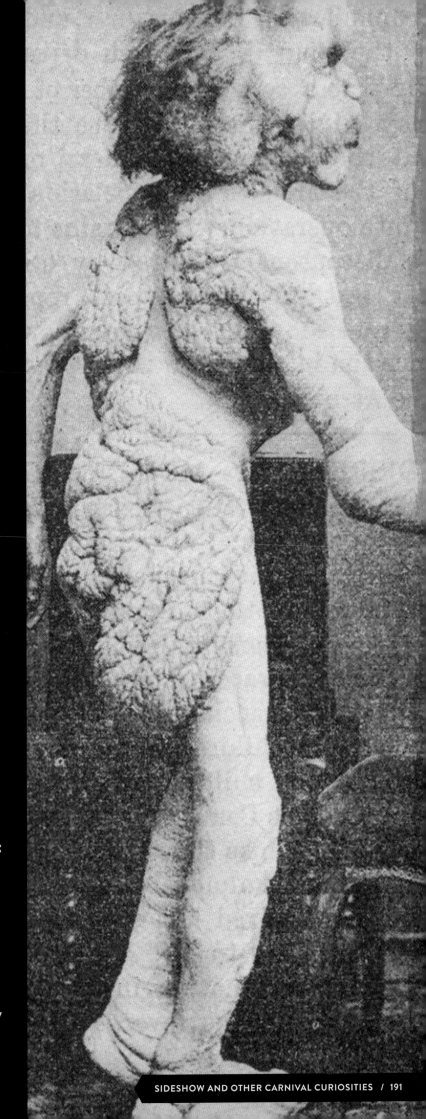

PHOTO CREDITS